Modern War: A Very Short Introduction

VERY SHORT INTRODUCTIONS are for anyone wanting a stimulating and accessible way in to a new subject. They are written by experts, and have been published in more than 25 languages worldwide.

The series began in 1995, and now represents a wide variety of topics in history, philosophy, religion, science, and the humanities. The VSI library now contains more than 300 volumes—a Very Short Introduction to everything from ancient Egypt and Indian philosophy to conceptual art and cosmology—and will continue to grow in a variety of disciplines.

Very Short Introductions available now:

ADVERTISING Winston Fletcher
AFRICAN HISTORY John Parker and
    Richard Rathbone
AGNOSTICISM Robin Le Poidevin
AMERICAN HISTORY Paul S. Boyer
AMERICAN IMMIGRATION
    David A. Gerber
AMERICAN POLITICAL PARTIES
    AND ELECTIONS L. Sandy Maisel
AMERICAN POLITICS Richard M. Valelly
THE AMERICAN PRESIDENCY
    Charles O. Jones
ANAESTHESIA Aidan O'Donnell
ANARCHISM Colin Ward
ANCIENT EGYPT Ian Shaw
ANCIENT GREECE Paul Cartledge
ANCIENT PHILOSOPHY Julia Annas
ANCIENT WARFARE Harry Sidebottom
ANGELS David Albert Jones
ANGLICANISM Mark Chapman
THE ANGLO-SAXON AGE John Blair
THE ANIMAL KINGDOM Peter Holland
ANIMAL RIGHTS David DeGrazia
THE ANTARCTIC Klaus Dodds
ANTISEMITISM Steven Beller
ANXIETY Daniel Freeman and
    Jason Freeman
THE APOCRYPHAL GOSPELS
    Paul Foster
ARCHAEOLOGY Paul Bahn
ARCHITECTURE Andrew Ballantyne
ARISTOCRACY William Doyle
ARISTOTLE Jonathan Barnes
ART HISTORY Dana Arnold

ART THEORY Cynthia Freeland
ATHEISM Julian Baggini
AUGUSTINE Henry Chadwick
AUSTRALIA Kenneth Morgan
AUTISM Uta Frith
THE AVANT GARDE David Cottington
THE AZTECS David Carrasco
BACTERIA Sebastian G. B. Amyes
BARTHES Jonathan Culler
BEAUTY Roger Scruton
BESTSELLERS John Sutherland
THE BIBLE John Riches
BIBLICAL ARCHAEOLOGY Eric H. Cline
BIOGRAPHY Hermione Lee
THE BLUES Elijah Wald
THE BOOK OF MORMON Terryl Givens
BORDERS Alexander C. Diener and
    Joshua Hagen
THE BRAIN Michael O'Shea
THE BRITISH CONSTITUTION
    Martin Loughlin
THE BRITISH EMPIRE Ashley Jackson
BRITISH POLITICS Anthony Wright
BUDDHA Michael Carrithers
BUDDHISM Damien Keown
BUDDHIST ETHICS Damien Keown
CANCER Nicholas James
CAPITALISM James Fulcher
CATHOLICISM Gerald O'Collins
THE CELL Terence Allen and Graham Cowling
THE CELTS Barry Cunliffe
CHAOS Leonard Smith
CHILDREN'S LITERATURE
    Kimberley Reynolds

Richard English

MODERN WAR

A Very Short Introduction

OXFORD
UNIVERSITY PRESS

OXFORD

UNIVERSITY PRESS

Great Clarendon Street, Oxford, OX2 6DP,
United Kingdom

Oxford University Press is a department of the University of Oxford.
It furthers the University's objective of excellence in research, scholarship,
and education by publishing worldwide. Oxford is a registered trade mark of
Oxford University Press in the UK and in certain other countries

Published in the United States of America by Oxford University Press
198 Madison Avenue, New York, NY 10016, United States of America

British Library Cataloguing in Publication Data
Data available

ISBN 978-0-19-960789-1

Printed and bound by
CPI Group (UK) Ltd, Croydon, CR0 4YY

For Maxine, Jasmine, and Arabella

Contents

Acknowledgements

Scholarly research and writing are not solitary endeavours, even for the fundamentally eremitical. It is a pleasure to record my own debt to those people who have made work on this book both possible and pleasurable. Colleagues and students at the University of St Andrews and (before that) at Queen's University, Belfast, provided intellectual stimulation and valuable comradeship. Scholars who invited me to deliver lectures on political violence over recent years, and audience members who engaged with my arguments when I did so, have greatly enriched my thinking on the subject of modern war. I am especially grateful to my hosts and interlocutors at the London School of Economics, Georgetown University, the University of California, San Diego, the University of Oxford, the Olympia Summer Seminars in Greece, the University of Copenhagen, the Oxford Literary Festival, the University of Birmingham, and the University of Glasgow. Invidious though it might be to list individual names, I owe particular debts to Roy Foster, David Eastwood, Louise Richardson, Charles Townshend, Adam Roberts, Harvey Whitehouse, Eli Berman, John Anderson, Gillian Duncan, Hilda McNae, Karin Fierke, Bruce Hoffman, Bruce Hunter, and Andrew Gordon. At OUP, Luciana O'Flaherty, Emma Ma, and Matthew Cotton combined rigour, insight, professionalism, and graciousness in a highly impressive manner; and the various

Reader Reports obtained by the Press were sharp-sighted and beneficial. But my most precious debt remains, as always, to Maxine, Jasmine, and Arabella and so to them—as ever—I dedicate what I write.

List of illustrations

Introduction

I have written this book with three central aims in mind.

First, it is intended to provide an accessible, authoritative introduction to the important and painful subject of modern war. The plan is to do this by answering a series of inter-linked and difficult questions. Definition: what is modern war? Causation: what causes modern wars to begin, why do people fight in them, and why do they end? Lived experience: what has the experience of modern war involved? Legacies: what have modern wars achieved?

Second, the book adumbrates a particular argument about the answers to these questions, based on the depressing disjunction between what we so often assume and think and claim about modern war, and its historical reality. What is frequently assumed to be modern in war evaporates on close interrogation. The alleged causes for wars beginning and ending often fail to match the actual reasons behind these developments, and the reasons for people's fighting in such wars often differ both from the ostensible claims made by or about such people, and also from the actual reasons for the wars occurring in any case. Much of what we expect, celebrate, commemorate, and remember regarding the experience and achievements of modern war bears only partially overlapping relation to historical reality, and wars' actual achievements greatly diverge from both the ostensible and the actual aims and justifications behind their initial eruption. Meanwhile, most of our attempts to set out prophylactic measures and structures against modern war have seemed (and continue to appear) frequently doomed to blood-spattered failure.

More catechism than chronicle, this book is therefore one which possesses a cumulative argument, and an argument engaging with large-scale historical and political issues. But it is also a book which, third and most briefly, suggests some possibly valuable approaches towards important future research in the field. *Modern War* is more about generating, than attempting to conclude, thoughtful debate. In particular, its argument that future scholarship should radically depart from the current instinct towards separating terrorism from war in our analysis, is one which is intended to jolt life into wider assessments of various kinds of politically motivated violence.

Overall, I hope that readers will simultaneously gain from all three aspects of the work—the introductory, the argumentative, and the agenda-setting—and that this book-length essay will stimulate further thought, study, argument, disagreement, research, and writing on the topic.

Previous books of mine have, in various ways, dealt with violent historical and contemporary conflicts (*Armed Struggle*; *Irish Freedom*; *Terrorism*); like them, this one has been produced as a work of political history. As such, it regards it as axiomatic that we cannot understand modern war without simultaneously understanding much else (including matters of nationalism, the state, religion, economics, and empire). War remains both the most dangerous threat faced by modern humanity, and also one of the key influences determining and shaping politics, economy, and society in the modern period.

As Michael Howard has pointed out, the history of war is 'more than the operational history of armed forces', involving as it does 'the study of entire societies. Only by studying their cultures could one come to understand what it was that they fought about and why they fought in the way that they did'; and, as scholars such as Vivienne Jabri have suggested, we cannot fully understand war if we divorce it from social relationships and from questions of power and community. War and politics are especially linked, politics being central both to the causes of and to the effects or achievements of war. In all of these senses, modern war is societal, involving and having powerful implications for social action.

Moreover, I argue that war and its associated phenomena can only be properly comprehended if we examine them through historical lenses. In the words of the greatest ever writer on the subject, Carl von Clausewitz (see Figure 1): 'Examples from history make everything clear, and furnish the best description of proof in the empirical sciences. This applies with more force to the Art of War than to any other'. I recognize that no single discipline—and certainly no single academic—can command the whole subject of war now in its entirety, given the multiple disciplinary contributions and literatures that have developed. Yet, though it also draws on a wide range of disciplinary literatures (political science, international relations, sociology, philosophy, anthropology, economics, theology, psychology, literary studies, law), *Modern War* is very much the work of a political historian, and as such it is written with a view to balancing the unique and contingent and localized with wider questions of family resemblance between cases; with a commitment to interrogating first-hand sources and explanatory models alike with intimacy and scepticism; with a clear eye towards the importance of chronology, the danger of anachronism, and the need to beware crude epoch-demarcation; and with a preference for the context-specific and the complex over the generalized, the inevitabilist, and the mono-dimensional.

1. Carl von Clausewitz, 1780–1831

Chapter 1
Definition

> Massacres of boys! That indeed is the essence of modern
> war. The killing off of the young
> > H. G. Wells, *Mr Britling Sees It Through* (1916)

Understanding the nature and dynamics of war is arguably one of the most important of scholarly and political challenges, and a book on such a subject should therefore begin with definitional precision. So what, in essence, is 'war'?

The *Shorter Oxford English Dictionary* offers various possibilities, including 'hostile contention by means of armed forces, carried on between nations, states, or rulers, or between parties in the same nation or state; the employment of armed forces against a foreign power or against an opposing party in the state'; 'a contest between armed forces carried on in a campaign or series of campaigns'; 'actual fighting; a battle, engagement'; 'the kind of operations by which the contention of armed forces is carried on; fighting as a department of activity, as a profession, or as an art'. This helpfully identifies important elements (mutual enmity, the role of armed groups, the practice of actual fighting), as does the *Chambers C20th Dictionary* definition of war as 'a state of conflict: a contest between states, or between parties within a state (civil war) carried on by arms: any long-continued struggle'.

Brilliant students of the subject have offered subtler, yet still very incisive, definitions. In Michael Howard's compelling description, war is 'a great socio-political activity, distinguished from all other activities by the reciprocal and legitimized use of purposeful violence to attain political objectives'. Clausewitz himself crucially defined war as 'an act of violence intended to compel our opponent to fulfil our will'.

As hinted in the definitions above, there exist many different *types* of war, sometimes overlapping with one another: inter-state war, civil war, revolutionary war, imperial war, counter-terrorist war, religious war, anti-colonial war, and so on. And even each of these sub-categories is itself open to considerable change over time, within this deeply Protean phenomenon.

Drawing on such ideas, let us for the purposes of this book suggest that war involves heterogeneous, organized, mutual enmity, and violence between armed groups, on more than a minor scale, carried out with political objectives, possessing socio-political dynamics, and focused on the exerting of power in order to compel opponents. (To complicate issues helpfully, some scholars have suggested that 'warfare' represents a sub-set of war itself, with warfare involving the practical carrying on of war, the actual fighting within it.)

If 'war' is problematic, then defining 'modern' might be judged more difficult still. War possesses very deep historical roots, as those familiar with the Bible know well, and if (as suggested by Sidebottom) 'ancient' war is considered to have existed 'between about 750 BC and AD 650' then it might seem important to find a way of defining what distinctively 'modern' war involves by way of contrast. Here too, however, the target of acceptable definition can seem elusive.

For when *does* 'modern' war actually begin? People have argued for a variety of major fault lines in the history of war, some focusing on changes between the mid-sixteenth and mid-seventeenth centuries, others on a longer period between 1500 and 1800, and others again on a specifically late-18th-century moment. Such variation might, perhaps, encourage scepticism about whether we can identify any particular moment at which 'modern' war emerged; close reflection on definitions of what is supposedly modern in war might possibly reinforce such a sceptical view.

For if 'modern' is taken to mean 'now existing', 'of or pertaining to the present and recent times; originating in the current age or period' (as in the *Shorter OED*), then it possesses little analytical value except in a chronological sense, as something which blandly frames a manageable and delineated period of human experience. Since both war and the date of reflection are constantly changing, one might as well—in this sense—use the terms 'recent' and/or 'contemporary' rather than modern. This is an important point, since there exists a danger that attributing inherent qualities or dynamics to 'modern' war involves a solipsism of the present. Will a scholar in the 26th century really allow our own past two hundred years, for example, to own the term 'modern'? (And such a future scholar might well consider us to have moved from solipsism to excessive narcissism by the time they found us claiming that our era was in fact *post*-modern.) Should we therefore decide that there is no sense of modern war which is justifiable and defensible except to imply something which is recent and/or contemporary?

Again, there are those who might suggest that the continuities existing across any historical fault line are so striking that ideas of 'modern' and 'pre-modern' war are just illusory anyway, and that change is too incremental and messy—and inheritances from the past are simply too great—to allow for effective epoch-delineation. So can we be confident that there is any clear fault line between the modern and the pre-modern in war, given the historical existence of such strong continuities across eras?

Some have suggested that the notion of technological change allows for a more definitive idea of what modern war encompasses. A strong case can be made that, in Martin van Creveld's phrasing, 'war is completely permeated by technology and governed by it'. The 16th-century gunpowder revolution clearly made a huge difference in terms of the mechanics of potential destruction, as did the 19th-century development of artillery. Similarly important was the creation—also in the 19th century—of extensive railway networks: this innovation allowed for transformed possibilities in moving troops around (evident in the 1861–5 American Civil War, for example). Weapons, materials, and forces themselves could be moved faster, with more effective communication, and much greater coordination, allowing for a far larger scale of operation than had previously been possible. The siege of Sevastopol in the mid-1850s during the Crimean War reflected the enlarged scale of warfare which was now rendered possible, the Allies firing 1,350,000 rounds of artillery ammunition during the engagement.

Clearly, there is no doubt that technological change has altered war very strikingly at times; as Paul Hirst pointed out, 'The *Dreadnought* of 1905 would have been all but incomprehensible to a sailor from the *Victory* of 1805' (see Figures 2 and 3). Even more dramatically, the development of nuclear weapons (pioneered by the United States) shaped late 20th-century superpower thinking about strategy; a terrifying stalemate emerged, in which these awful weapons were judged too mutually destructive to use after the Second World War. But do such technological changes necessarily mean that one can identify a moment at which the 'modern' was inaugurated in war? It might rather be that there have emerged a series of irregularly, incrementally advancing aspects of much war-related technology. The tank, the computer, the radio, the machine gun, the aircraft, or the nuclear bomb could all be seen to have had a *potentially* decisive effect. But it is not easy to prove that technological change made war in 1850 more different from what it had been in 1750,

THE "VICTORY" AT PORTSMOUTH.

2. *HMS Victory, c.*1805

3. *HMS Dreadnought, c.*1905

than it was from what it was to become by 1950; or that the shift from 1950 to 2050 will need to be judged any less definitive.

Do tactics and scale help us to a greater extent? Again, there have been very clear continuities over surprisingly long periods. Close-quarter fighting remained on the battlefield in the early 19th century as it had been in the early sixteenth. And, while some might see large standing armies as definitive of modern war, their creation lay in the late 17th century; Wallenstein apparently possessed more than 100,000 men in the 1620s; and even the Persian army invading Greece in 480 BC had in it very large numbers of men. Even in terms of mass casualties, the picture is far from clear, when we set the blood-stained cataclysms of the First and Second World Wars in a comparative context which takes into account the proportion of existing world population killed or maimed in earlier conflicts.

Is there perhaps an *administrative* moment when the modern emerges in war? The effective professionalization of war in the 19th century certainly represented a major shift, with the more centralized, territorially powerful states of that period enjoying a capacity to direct and mobilize on a new basis. And if there is one leading contender for the prize of defining the modern moment in war, it perhaps is the ideological change which lay behind the making of so many latter-day states: namely, the emergence of nationalism as such in the late 18th century. I have argued elsewhere (in my book, *Irish Freedom*) that the essence of nationalism lies in a particularly powerful interweaving of the phenomena of community, struggle, and power, and that the emancipation derived from the intersection of equality, popular sovereignty, and freedom helped to create in the 18th century a new phenomenon (nationalism) on the foundations of a prior, powerful, and often constraining proto-nation.

The implications of this for our understanding of war are potentially profound, and they probably offer us the most meaningful basis for suggesting something inherently different about 'modern' war beyond its mere recentness.

For if there was one epochal transformation which produced genuinely, distinctively modern war, something qualitatively different from what had come before, then it is probably the French Revolution and the associated emergence of nationalism. The Revolution produced a nation capable of organizing self-consciously *as such* for war—effectively, for a national war, with a national economy geared towards this end and with forces which related to the struggle in a qualitatively different manner.

Mechanically, recruitment could now be effected on both a different scale and with a different type of soldier: there were more people involved, and their engagement in the process of war could be seen as possessing a new kind of commitment, given their equal share in the sovereignty which overarched their struggle. With mass mobilization and sustained professional militaries on a national basis, a new kind of armed force—a national force of potential patriots, with a national-political duty and freedom, on the basis of collective national resources—could be produced.

The 1793 introduction of the *levée en masse* effectively introduced conscription, decreeing that until the enemies of France had been expelled from the country, all of the nation's unmarried men and childless widowers between the ages of eighteen and twenty-five could be drawn into military service (Figure 4). By 1794 he therefore had over a million men in arms, a truly unprecedented European military force and systematic mobilization. This had both an ideological and a practical dimension: there was the need for more soldiers, but also a need to reflect the claim that the state embodied the general national and communal will, and to express this in the most practical manner. The June 1793 constitution in France gave all French

4. Napoleon Bonaparte, 1769–1821

men (there remained then what would now seem unacceptable gender limitations) the right to vote, and imposed on them all the duty of military service. In practice, of course, not all men would serve: not all Frenchmen became soldiers, and not all countries immediately introduced conscription (history does not step forward in a synchronized line like the Arsenal back-four of the early 1990s). But the idea of a different relationship between the individual and military commitment, communal loyalty, and duty had been established, with very powerful implications for the nature and scale and management of much subsequent—and distinctively modern—war.

Similarly, when the Prussian conscription law of 1814 decreed that defence of the country was a universal obligation, it represented both a national requirement (should the state require your services) and also a means of unifying the nation. This dual quality—both reflecting and reinforcing the change towards nationalism as a determining human force—lies at the heart of what might be seen as the most distinctive feature of an expressly modern form of war. Arguably, indeed, the character of war had changed fundamentally and enduringly. Nor were such changes merely European; Mehmet Ali, Viceroy of Egypt, introduced conscription in the 1820s, along with a military staff college in 1825.

There are more oblique ways, perhaps, of trying to define what is inherently distinctive about modern war. The historian might, for example, suggest that what most separates it from previous periods is the utterly different range, extent, weight, and type of evidence which we possess in relation to the phenomenon. To write about the early-21st-century Iraq War, as opposed to the kind of war on which Thucydides so brilliantly focused, is arguably to engage in a different species of analysis, because of the respectively so different kinds of source-lens through which one can and must view the objects of study.

Yet again, there are scholars who have parcelled the history of war into further sub-units which threaten somewhat to undermine the importance of 'modern' war, as such, in any case. Those adhering to a four-generations paradigm, for instance, set out a strong case for notions of war as divided into the First Generation (horse and musket, Napoleonic wars), the Second Generation (rifle and railway, from the American Civil War until the First World War), the Third Generation (blitzkrieg/fast-manoeuvre warfare), and the Fourth Generation (asymmetric warfare, deploying information technologies; insurgent-focused, involving political-economic-social networks as well as the military; evident in the 21st-century wars in Afghanistan and Iraq). Has a recent Revolution in Military Affairs (RMA), indeed, rendered much 'modern' war redundant? Proponents of such an idea suggest that, in a post-Cold War context, information technology has transformed war in ways which leave many types of conventional military force near-obsolete, as intelligence-gathering, sophisticated communications systems, the deployment of small forces, and the use of precision-directed weapons have replaced their prior centrality.

Yet others again have espoused a 'new wars' thesis, suggesting that during the 1980s and 1990s there emerged a new kind of organized violence, effectively a new kind of war. The latter supposedly involved a blurring of the line between inter-state/inter-group violence, crime, and large-scale human rights abuses; these 'new wars' were presented as emerging against the background of a dislocating globalization, and as bearing a strong imprint from international, transnational, and diasporic influences; they were more concerned than were previous wars with identity politics, rather than with goals of an ideological or territorial kind; they were also supposedly fought differently, with violence being more deliberately and definitively directed against civilians; they were differently financed, in a less centralized and more criminalized manner, and they were characterized by the fragmentation of the state. New wars represented, in leading advocate Mary Kaldor's phrasing, 'a mixture of war, crime, and human rights violations'.

I myself am sceptical about how new such wars actually were and are. There is nothing historically new about large-scale, war-time violence deliberately targeted against civilians; nor are crime, or violence organized by criminals in warfare, new aspects of modern war (regrettably); it is also true that identity politics have long formed a part of modern war, well before the 1980s; and—to the historically minded—the fragmentation of state authority in war settings is a very familiar sight. Moreover, a powerful body of other scholarly work now supports such scepticism (including that contained in Malesevic, and in Strachan and Scheipers).

So where do all these countervailing arguments about 'modern' war leave us? It still seems to me that an historically decisive change did occur in the long late 18th-century moment, one which was of such high importance that it makes sense to speak afterwards of something distinctively new and effectively modern about war. I have alluded more than once already to the great Carl von

Clausewitz (1780–1831), the Prussian soldier-philosopher whose posthumous classic, *On War*, presented the phenomenon as comprising three key elements whose interaction determined its enduring character: these were violence, chance, and politics. Clausewitz sagely pointed to the manner in which 'friction' (the difficulties and obstacles which in practice, contingently, and often in unanticipated and unintended manner resisted one's purpose, and made the seemingly easy very difficult to accomplish) produced the lived outcome of conflict. He asserted that war, properly understood, was a rational instrument of national policy—a military means to a political end: 'War is a mere continuation of policy by other means', 'a political instrument', 'an instrument of policy'; 'War can never be separated from political intercourse'.

As noted, Clausewitz presented war as involving coercive power on an enduring basis:

> If our opponent is to be made to comply with our will, we must place him in a situation which is more oppressive to him than the sacrifice which we demand; but the disadvantages of this position must naturally not be of a transitory nature, at least in appearance, otherwise the enemy, instead of yielding, will hold out, in the prospect of a change for the better.

But, for our discussion of the modern, it is also telling that he considered the French Revolution (against whose forces he had himself fought) to have inaugurated an era in which a different relationship existed between the individual and war: war could now truly be rational, instrumental, *and also national* in a way which meant that its organization was on a different basis, and that its fighters related to it in a more integral manner, than had previously been the case. With the emergence of modern nationalism, modern war was born; and if one genuinely did consider the intersection of equality, sovereignty, and freedom to determine one's political world, then fighting for the nation changed the nature of war historically.

'Modern war', therefore, can be defined as heterogeneous, organized, mutual enmity and violence between armed groups, on more than a minor scale, carried out with political objectives, possessing socio-political dynamics, and focused on the exerting of power in order to compel opponents; it is located in the post-French Revolutionary era of nationalism, during which the interwoven dynamics of national community, struggle, and power have determined a particular form of violent conflict.

'Strategy' and 'tactics' must be tied together in definition, I think, so we will define the former as the art of using military means to achieve specific political ends and policy objectives, and the latter as operating at a lower level: tactics constitute the detailed, day-to-day choices involved in using organized, armed forces in line with strategic aims. Thus defined, tactics involve the operationalizing of strategy. As so often, Clausewitz puts it best: 'tactics is the theory of the use of military forces in combat. Strategy is the theory of the use of combats for the object of the war', and 'the employment of the battle as the means towards the attainment of the object of the War'.

Chapter 2
Causation

> History teaches that somewhere behind every war there are
> always a few lies used as justifications...Somewhere behind
> every war there are always a few founding lies.
>
> Mark Kurlansky, *Non-Violence* (2006)

What causes modern wars to begin? Clearly, no single answer or
model can successfully account for the contingent commencement
of all of them. The various kinds of war under scrutiny might—
across category (civil war, inter-state war, revolutionary war, and
so on), location, time period, scale—require very different types of
explanation; and the body of data one decides to analyse can
determine the kind of answer that one is likely to reach in terms of
the causation behind the violence. Yet, historically, certain central
themes do suggest themselves as potentially significant and
repeated and, while wars have had myriad origins, we will
consider here the often inter-linked roles of nationalism, the state,
empire, religion, and economics. This reflects our earlier
observation that the proper understanding of modern war will
relate it to wider forces of politics and society, recognizing that
there is far more than the merely military involved.

Does nationalism cause war? There are those who assume that it
frequently does, on the ground that ancient national hatreds

provide a fuel which people find it hard lastingly to resist burning. But there are brilliant scholars, such as David Laitin, who dispute this popular view, pointing out that the vast majority of neighbouring ethnic groups do not, for example, resort to violent conflict. Perhaps, therefore, there is little necessary connection between ethnic or national difference and the generation of warfare. We might, as Nobel-Prize-winning psychologist Daniel Kahneman has pointed out, be falling victim here to the availability heuristic: the tendency to abstract general arguments from an unrepresentative sample of salient, highly noticeable, easily remembered cases. We notice and report when national or ethnic groups resort to war and bloodshed; it is far less noticeable when (as in the far larger number of cases) they coexist peacefully with one another.

But even if there is no automatically causal relationship between nationalism and war (and I think that there is not), rival nationalisms do frequently appear to be at least involved in war's creation; and I think it is possible to explain some of the dynamics which have led, on historical occasion, from the nationalistic to the commencement of war. The thing to focus on is what it is in the causation of war which it specifically takes nationalism to explain, and that means that we have to be very clear about this most important of modern phenomena: to consider closely the definition and dynamics of nationalism itself. We will return soon to the practical implications of this for modern war; but it is necessary first to examine this most important phenomenon—nationalism—in a little detail, in order to grasp what is really happening (and why) when many wars commence.

There are difficulties enough in defining the words 'nation' (a body of people thinking themselves a distinct group characterized by shared descent, history, and culture), 'national' (something distinctively characteristic of a nation), and 'nationality' (the fact of belonging to a nation, or the identity or feeling related to it).

Defining 'nationalism' itself is an even more complex process, but my own scholarly argument has been that the true definition and explanation of nationalism lie in a particular interweaving of the politics of community, struggle, and power.

The nationalist idea of community—arguably our most powerful yet—resonates with many of humanity's deepest instincts and needs: towards survival, security, protection, and safety; towards the fulfilment of economic and other practical needs; towards necessary belonging and, in particular (for our inherently sociable species), a belonging to stable, coherent, meaningful, lastingly special, and distinctive groups.

For this process of belonging to work, we require shared means of communication between members of the group, things that provide the basis for durable agreement, coherence, interaction, integration, and trust. These can take various forms, and are often enough very practical as well as possessing emotional or psychological value. They include *territory*: the attachment to our own special place, to a land on which we work, on whose resources we rely, and from whose distinctive features we derive emotional and practical sustenance. To the centrality of place and national homeland might be added the pivotal communal feature of the *people* themselves. There are practical dimensions here, since community with those around us is required for our survival. But there are psychological rewards also, because the ennobling of our own special people allows for enhanced individual self-worth, fulfilment, purpose, and meaning.

Nationalists often take this further with notions of communal *descent*. As members of the same nation, so the assumption goes, we are linked by blood. This may be only partly true (since national groups are not hermetically sealed units of descent, but tend rather to be much more hybrid phenomena); but, as such, it is clearly not entirely untrue. The people to whom you are born, frequently do determine your national identity; and you are indeed more likely to be related by blood to more members of your own nation than you are to those of another.

Through much of this, wider linkages of *culture* represent another means of communication and another explanation of why nationalist community so appeals. This can involve a distinctively shared language, but also metaphorical languages of religion or music or sport or diet or value, which allow for shared interaction and trust and meaning within a national group. And the key feature here is our own national culture's perceived specialness.

Tied in with shared culture is often a reliance on a sense of shared *history*. This group to which we belong is a lasting one; it has gained worth through its historic achievements and legacies, and has purpose and direction in its imagined future. If national history has reached a low point, then we are united in a sense of the powerful need for historic redemption. There is potentially great appeal in such historical stories, containing compelling lessons and morals.

And so the national community tends also to have an *ethical* dimension. Our group is not merely typical in what it embodies, but is characterized rather by superior moral claims, values, purposes, and obligations. A darker feature of nationalist community—but again one which both defines and explains its appeal—is to be found in the idea of *exclusiveness*: what you specially are, implies and requires a category of what you are definitely not. If my national culture and history define who is within my community, then they also define who is outside, beyond, and excluded from it. And this too can appeal to many people: in telling a tale of good-versus-evil, and in providing great comfort and moral certainty at the same time.

National communities do not require all of these features—shared attachments to territory, people, descent, culture, history, ethics, and exclusivism—but they do require some of them, and the emotional and practical logic within each of these features helps to explain the existence, durability, appeal, and pervasiveness of such communal, national groups.

Yet nationalism involves more than membership of such self-conscious community. It also involves struggle: collective mobilization, activity, movement towards change and a programmatic striving for goals. Such goals can vary, including sovereign independence, secession from a larger political unit, the survival or rebirth of national culture, the realization of economic advantage for the national group, and much more throughout history. And, again, overlapping motivations can be detected. There is the central urge towards self-preservation; the practical pursuit of material interests; the longing for dignity, prestige, or meaning; the explicable response to threats (actual or perceived); the urge to avenge past wrongs and to rectify group grievance.

In all of this, nationalist struggle involves the putting right of what is perceivedly wrong in the present; and, in all of this, there is also an individual engagement with the organized pursuit of communal goals, with communal advantage benefiting the individual nationalist in ways which help to explain nationalism's enduringly wide appeal.

If the rewards for the individual are magnified by involvement in nationalist collectivity here, then it is also worth noting the dual allure of nationalist struggle. There is the instrumental appeal (struggle as a means of achieving worthwhile and necessary goals). But there is also the attraction inherent in struggle itself (with its psychological rewards, and with its conferring upon individual and group alike of the very qualities so sought, prized, and cherished by the nationalist movement).

How do nationalists pursue such struggle? Sometimes through violence (in wars of national liberation, expansion, or annexation, deeply relevant to the themes of this book); sometimes through electoral and party-political process; sometimes through cultural campaigns; sometimes through the embedding of national ideas in repeated rituals and routines, and in the emblems built into national life and place.

But nationalism is about, not merely community in struggle, but also and centrally about questions of power. Power is what is so frequently sought by nationalists (very often in the form of a state which matches the nation); and the deployment of power in pursuit of nationalist objectives defines—and again, I think, helps to explain—nationalist activity. It might even be suggested that, at root, nationalism is really a politics *of* legitimizing power. Nationalists tend to assume the nation to be the appropriate source of political authority, and therefore to seek power for their own distinctive national community. The legitimacy of national power involves the attractive prospect of those in power in your community being like yourself, coming from your own national group, and representing your own interests and values and preferences and instincts.

And nationalist ideas about power focus on the vital notion of sovereignty. Indeed, much of the appeal of nationalism lies in this attachment to the idea of the national community possessing full sovereignty over itself as a free and independent unit. All people within the nation share equally in the sovereign power which makes decisions for the group, and so any law derives ultimately from your own authority. Central to nationalism's appeal is this very idea, that by sharing equally in the power which governs us, we are made truly, lastingly free. As nationalists, we give consent to our national rulers and to their possession of sovereign power; and such individual attachment to the idea of popular national sovereignty seems to make a certain sense because we, as individuals within the national community, have an equal share in the sovereignty through which decisions are made for us. As such, we are supposedly liberated.

This is why state power and self-determination lie so close to the heart of nationalist histories and politics around the world, and why freedom is so closely associated with nationalism in so many people's minds and struggles. But if power is the objective and the explanation of so much nationalist struggle, then power too lies at the heart of what it is that nationalists actually do, in their day-to-day and year-to-year activities. Power is deployed by nationalist communities in their pursuit, achievement, and maintenance of objectives; power is used as leverage in nationalist campaigns for the righting of wrongs, for the winning or defending of freedom or culture; power can be wielded in violent, propagandistic, intimidatory, administrative, verbal, literary, state, sub-state, and many other forms of persuasion and coercion. This involves widespread mobilization rather than merely individual acts; and the attraction of wielding such power helps to explain the durable appeal of nationalism as part of one's way of life.

So community, struggle, and power offer the interwoven definition and explanation of nationalism and its extraordinary dominance in politics and history. It is not that we cannot find other means of identifying and belonging, or of pursuing change and acquiring power. The point is rather this: that the particular interweaving of community, struggle, and power in the form of nationalism, offers far grander opportunities than do these other means. The family cannot offer the scale of interaction to provide for our necessary exchange or safety; even a very powerful job will tend not to allow for access to the kind of serious, sustained power available through nationalism; and sub-national cultural enthusiasm— whether for region, or football team, or whatever—will not allow for such large-scale, durable, all-inclusive possibilities for getting what we deeply want, as will the national.

Indeed, nationalism has an absorptive quality, which allows it to subsume and incorporate and gain further strength from other areas of our life in ways which seem to strengthen them too. The family offers comfort and meaning and belonging, but is protected by the power of the national community; the interests of the business are defended and furthered by the nation; sporting enthusiasm or musical pride gain distinction and exaltation through their national dimensions. While feminism, socialism, or religion can all appeal very powerfully, none of them can absorb the nation in the way that nationalism can absorb them. In so many people's eyes, despite its many failings, nationalism has seemed to offer a better set of possibilities than its rival kinds of world view.

Now, if community, struggle, and power do between them explain nationalism, what then is the relation of this to the causation of war? I think the link is often absolutely vital. If the intensity of individual and collective commitment to national community is explicable in terms of the precious priorities involved (security, survival, social meaning, distinctiveness), then the rational and emotional force towards protecting such community from enemy threats might seem supremely compelling and ethically demanding, even through war. The elements of precious territory, people, culture, and proud history—reinforced by a driving sense of ethical rectitude and exclusivist assumption—make for a repeatedly powerful cocktail in potential conflict situations, and can provide the basis for thinking of, and actually, going to war.

The inherent and instrumental aspects of the appeal of nationalist struggle also help to explain why resorting to the awfulness of war might seem to so many people to be reasonable and appealing. Movement towards achieving what is necessary through the only possible (violent) methods—whether the necessary involves material or other gain or acquisition from others, or the protection or securing of power for people representative of yourself—again makes sense of the dynamics of otherwise seemingly strange nationalist imperatives towards vile blood-spilling. At its root, there often lies the central allure of the intersection of sovereignty, equality, and freedom: its pursuit, and its defence once achieved, have often seemed to legitimate and necessitate warfare through modern history—effectively, to give a purpose to war.

Nationalism allows therefore for those simultaneous processes of causation which are instrumental, rational, emotional, expressive, and intuitive. The viscerally, vengefully destructive and the calculatingly calibrated can coexist within this capacious framework, and they have often done so in practice. Grievance-driven nationalism, and its communal, struggling dynamics, between them do explain the impulse so often towards the generating of war.

None of this is to say that nationalism automatically or inevitably produces war, or that the process involves nationalism alone. But the causal possibility has been too evident throughout modern history for it to be ignored, not least because of the ethical power which nationalist claims frequently possess—that national and state boundaries should be congruent with each other, for instance. And it is complemented by the fact that nationalism emerges from and reinforces forms of large-scale organization and identification which can also facilitate the emergence of war in the modern era. With a participatory sense of military obligation, it was possible on a national basis to establish standing armies; as alluded to earlier, the French Revolutionary fault line is significant in regard to the modernity of war, and conscription is emblematic here in relation to the capacity for such warfare to be waged in practice: spectacularly, between 1800 and 1815 Napoleon drafted over two million men.

There is also a justificatory level to the relationship between nationalism and war's emergence. Even if one were sceptical about the causal case laid out above (that the dynamics of large-scale community, struggle, and power at work in nationalism have on occasion been the contingent basis for the generation of specific wars), there is no doubt that nationalism has been used powerfully in many instances to *justify* and mobilize support for going to war.

Indeed, the often-noted paradox of nationalisms' ubiquity and their simultaneously local uniqueness provides an unrivalled opportunity for the near-global, yet also the locally particularistic, legitimation of going to war.

This justification can be cast in very particular terms indeed—defending specific communities, distinctive ways of life, individual towns, villages, and cultures—and the fact that the nationalistic has so often been earlier embedded in such a way as to make it seem utterly natural, can make it appear less jarring to fight, kill, and die for its cause. Although it is very often the actual, rather than the imagined, community for which one goes into combat, the extensive reach allowed for by that greater association renders modern war far more easily initiated. Ideological legitimations rarely come more powerful than the nationalistic, nor do they often have as wide a reach: wrongs to be avenged, threats to be averted, honour to be upheld, just demands to be pursued—all have historically been evident in the stories we have told ourselves in justification of our contingent bellicosity.

Such justifications might only partly overlap with the genuine, historical causes behind the war, but the part played can none the less be decisive, giving a pervasive and plausible rationale to which so many people can subscribe. Moreover, such a process only works when nationalistic claims resonate with what many in the relevant nation consider to be authentic and powerful, rather than factitious. Nations may be invented but—as with other inventions—their creators are constrained by the ingredients available to them, and by the inherited limitations upon the ways in which these ingredients will interact with each other and with individuals in community.

This is not to say that nationalism causes wars in any necessary or crude or simple way. Stathis Kalyvas's important work powerfully cautions against any casual assumption that pre-war loyalties might serve as a neat explanation for why civil wars, for example, begin, or for why people fight in them once they have done so. Often, local dynamics trump the alleged master division in a civil war conflict, the local rather than the national determining and defining what actually takes place in the context of such wars.

But amid the terrible range of different wars in the modern era, there can be little doubt that nationalism has frequently played some causal role, and nor is it impossible to detect rational calculation behind this on occasion. Even admitting Kalyvas's cautionary argument, national self-determination does still appear to be one of the major causes for modern civil wars. And, as noted, it is not hard to see why: nationalism holds an explicable, very deep appeal, and rival claims about boundaries and which 'self' should do the 'determining' have generated some of the most salient modern conflicts. Moreover, the fusing of the national and the bellicose can become deeply, enduringly interwoven into particular culture and memory. Bismarck, the mythical father of the German nation-state, was one whose lasting influence drew together very intimately the martial and the proudly nationalistic.

One subtle argument about why, in settings of contested self-determination, regimes do decide to fight in wars has been offered by Barbara Walter, who claims that states frequently have rational bases for fighting would-be seceders, in order to deter future insurgency against the integrity and forces of the existing state. To fight against challengers, rather than to grant them what they demand, is to build a reputation for toughness—a reputation which might then put off potential challengers in the future by demonstrating the high and violent costs to be paid for rebelling. Considered strategically (with strategy being the art of using military means to achieve specific political ends and policy objectives), with an eye to possible future challengers who possess similar grievances, it might be judged rational to fight rather than to yield, especially when such instincts are reinforced by political pressures from other sections of one's own constituency, and by ideological commitments, and by historical inheritances, and by economic considerations and the importance of holding on to valuable resources.

Interwoven with nationalism, in many instances, has been the role of the state. Despite some robust challengers from above and from below, states remain central to the explanation of international relations, international order, and international politics, and their drive towards both survival and power often seems very clear. In this sense, states might be seen as reinforcing the tendencies alluded to above regarding nationalisms, as the instinct towards defence, expansion, and rivalrous competition contributes towards generating actual warfare. Threatened, hedged in, facing threats to their sovereignty, and fearing imminent danger, states have often engaged in what Hobbes would have considered a pre-emptive, yet ultimately defensive, first strike against their enemies. Why do states go to war in the modern period? This Hobbesian, pre-emptive, defensive, self-preserving, first-strike aggression offers one important answer. State rulers might frequently be wrong about the extent of the threat which they actually face (possessing, as they do, imperfect information); and they might be misguided in thinking that pre-emptive aggression forms their best defence anyway. But the mismatch between perception and historical reality has been at the heart of much of the story of modern war.

Does the precise *nature* of the modern state cause war? The vast literature on the phenomenon has carried within it lasting battles over definition, and attempts to separate functional from structural definitions of 'the state' will probably fail: serious consideration of what the state is, in terms of institutional structures, will necessarily involve interrogation of the intended, perceived, or actual functions of the different bodies involved, and the reverse is equally true. For our purposes here (and consistent with a definition which Charles Townshend and I offered in an earlier book on the issue), the state will be considered 'an independent political society (within a system of other such societies), recognized as exercising sovereignty over a given territory, and vindicating that sovereignty in the face of external and internal challenges; a political entity with the power to regulate individuals and organizations within its territory, successfully claiming a monopoly on legitimate force and recognized by its population as legitimate; an organization (or co-ordinated and relatively centralized set of organizations) with military, legislative, administrative, judicial, and governmental functions; and a political entity relating fundamentally to the maintenance of order within its territory and to the business of government, with the latter role involving institutions marked by their public and impersonal quality'.

Now each of these elements can be seen to provide some occasion or basis for violent conflict: to achieve or protect independence and sovereignty against rivals; to alter or sustain territorial boundaries; to enforce regulatory or coercive rights (or to resist them); to uphold or subvert order maintenance; and to express a failure of collective legitimation. Moreover, the very qualities of the modern state also make modern war more feasible, whether in terms of an intersection with popular, national engagement, or in terms of the practical capacity for organization and sustenance of the actual violence. The ability to carry out war in the modern period, and on the large-scale, organized, sustained basis that has (regrettably) been so possible, depends upon the mechanical apparatus of the state. As Sinisa Malesevic has suggested, some of this involves the intersection of state bureaucracy with organized coercion, and relies on the money-raising, centralized, organizational capacities possessed. In reality, the possibility of mass, effective mobilization depends in substantial measure upon the modern state.

Yet counter-arguments can be offered too. If states make modern war possible then the reverse might also be claimed: that it was war which made possible the modern state, and that the causal path is historically not, therefore, straightforward or unilinear. If rulers required finance in order to prosecute war, then raising taxes from the population became alluring, and organization towards the modern state and its bureaucracies ensued.

More importantly, reflection on our definition of the state explains why so often this formation has worked historically *against* war's generation too. Consensually-based legitimacy within accepted territorial boundaries; the autonomous political expression of the interwoven nationalist goods of equality, sovereignty, and freedom; the provision of stability and order and protection; the sustained basis for economic organization and success; legal and administrative structures which help to avoid enduring chaos; the sustenance of impersonal structures which allow for maximal opportunity among the wider population—all of these goods have been effectively ensured by many modern states, helping to render less likely the eruption of violent conflict.

Indeed, in terms of the production of *civil* wars, it has been powerfully argued that the key variable is precisely the weakness or otherwise of the state. Where a state is (in David Laitin's words) 'unable to provide basic services to its population, unable to police its peripheries, and unable to distinguish law abiders from lawbreakers', then such weak states are more likely to prompt the emergence of civil war. If we want to prevent civil war, such arguments suggest, what we need are strong states, able and keen to enforce the rule of law effectively. On such readings, it is state failure, rather than anything necessarily inherent in the state as such, which actually prompts war to start.

This is not to suggest that states are inherently oriented towards peace, but rather to caution against an assessment which leans too far towards associating the nature of the state with the production of war. There have been and remain cases where the perceived mismatch between nation and state has generated violent conflict; and there have historically been many arguments (classically

Marxist ones among them) which have presented the necessity of the violent overthrow and takeover of the state as part of its true historical trajectory. In practice, this has often involved revolutionary movements attempting to usurp by force the power of those states which have politically and violently oppressed them. In his excellent study of the Cold War version of this phenomenon, Jeff Goodwin stresses the political dynamics involved, focusing valuably on state actions, practices, and structures and the ways in which these sometimes form, shape, or prompt their anti-state revolutionary enemies. When states sustain an unpopular cultural, economic, or social order; when they exclude mobilized groups from power or resources; when they use repressive violence against their opponents; when they lack effective policing or infrastructural capacity; and when they embody corrupt or arbitrary rule—then, Goodwin argues, revolutionary movements can be and have been created and shaped in response. Of course, such state-centred perspectives alone cannot explain everything, and nor does Goodwin claim that they do. But these dynamics of state action and reaction, and the problem generated when mobilized groups are denied sufficient space for political efficacy and non-violent change, have historically played their part in generating revolutionary, insurgent war.

Does the nature of the international state *system* also sometimes cause wars to commence? Contingent failures of diplomacy, and the domino effect of alliances, might be seen as contributing to the brutal narrative here. But has the nature of the system within which such contingencies emerge determined the degree of their unfortunate likelihood?

Some subtlety is required here. In a brilliantly revisionist critique, Professor David Lake has argued that, contrary to International Relations scholarly orthodoxy, the international system is far from purely anarchic, and far from lacking in authority structures. In fact, he asserts, the hierarchical authority (legitimate, rightful rule) of some states over others (mutually accepted by the dominant partner and the subsidiary partner in the hierarchy) provides the clue to understanding much in the way of state action and interaction in the modern era, including warfare. There exists a relational, self-enforcing, and asymmetrical power contract or bargain between states, between the ruler and the ruled, regarding security and economics. So dominant State A provides subordinate State B with beneficial political order (the protection of people, property, territory, and so forth), and in turn receives from State B a duty of compliance with its commands, as well as the right to rule. Subordinate State B provides State A with legitimacy, compliance, and the right to rule (and State A will also benefit from international order, of course), and in turn receives order (protection of person, property, and the like being effectively maintained). Both parties therefore think themselves better off in this relationship than they would be without it, and to benefit mutually.

What does this analysis of state relationships mean for our understanding of modern war? It perhaps explains why some states do in fact go to war (State A doing so in order to aid subordinate State B, to come to State B's assistance in a dispute as its protector and defender; State B joining a conflict in order to join the dominant state, and necessarily following it into war). So the USA, since the mid-20th century, has enjoyed hierarchy over many subordinate states, with great effect on its subordinates' respective relationships to warfare. But this paradigm also helps explain why states have *not* gone to war or militarily intervened, since these mutually beneficial, internally peaceful hierarchies often render such clashes self-damaging by contrast. Lake's thesis asserts the existence of a subtler mechanism for control and state relations than the assumption of simple coercion, while avoiding the ahistorical assumption of utterly contingent anarchy.

Hierarchy might be seen as a kind of decaffeinated form of empire, and long before modern wars erupted—as far back at least as Sparta's 5th-century BC struggle to challenge the Athenian empire in the Peloponnesian War—the relationship between empire and the creation of violent conflict has been a difficult one to disentangle. Wars have been fought to create empires, to augment them, to defend them, to subvert them, and to prevent someone else from having them. These processes can be fuelled by an aggressively expansionist ideology (communism, fascism), and can also be clothed in comforting self-justifications which only partly overlap with real motivation and cause, empires often being justified on the supposedly legitimizing grounds of bringing benefits to the receiver, whether a species of religious faith, or economic advantage, or civilization, or progress, or democracy, or human rights. As so often, the relationship between rationalization and underlying reason is messy here rather than neat. And the different and rival tellings of war will rarely vary as sharply as they do when apologists for an empire, and those ruled under the imperium, respectively take to the podium.

The British Empire, to consider one powerful example, emerged and expanded through a mixture of trade and war; to protect its trading operations, it was necessary to defend them against rivals. War could not sustain empire on its own; collaboration and many complex motives for acquiescence were required for that. But it did play its part in generating and defending imperial power. Likewise, as hinted earlier, and as argued strongly by Barbara Walter, there might be a compelling logic in imperial rulers deciding to fight rather than to cede power to their subjects, since the signalling of a willingness to resist one challenger might be taken to represent a necessary statement in prevention of the disintegration of imperial integrity, something arguably evident in the UK's response to the Boers during 1899–1902, and in 1916–22 revolutionary Ireland (and within the context that well over four hundred million people lived under British rule at the start of the First World War). Inter-imperial rivalry can form the decisive impetus towards war (as in Crimea in the 1850s); wars of liberation represent another element of the pattern (Palestine

1946–8, Indo-China 1947–53 and 1964–75, Kenya 1953–8, Algeria 1955–62, Cyprus 1959–60, Aden 1963–7, and so on); while the actual break-up of empire can lead to post-imperial warfare also, as in the case of Indian-Pakistani conflicts in the post-British era.

India and Pakistan have fought each other three times since the partition of 1947, the first occasion prompted by the issue of the largely Muslim Kashmir region in the first place joining India rather than Pakistan. India was utterly resistant to Kashmiri self-determination, and the Kashmiri problem has remained a painful one between the two great states. The 1947–8 war was followed by a cease-fire line which held, with minor changes after the 1965 war, until the 1971 war—at which point another line was established. Post-imperial, boundary-related conflict here involved also, therefore, the politics of state integrity, and the force of rival, religiously-inflected nationalisms. And the problem has continued to endure: in 1989 a separatist uprising began in Kashmir; India was furious at this violence and at alleged Pakistani support for the separatists behind it; for its part, Pakistan was angry about supposed human rights violations by Indian forces against Muslims.

I am not claiming either that imperial urges on their own explain the emergence of wars, nor that the ambiguous economic and other benefits of empire have been such as to make imperial advantage worth the effort and cost of warfare anyway. But the dynamics and legacies of empire—albeit interwoven with some of our other major forces—have helped to explain the onset of many wars.

The Kashmiri illustration also highlights another major potential causal force behind the generation of war, namely that of religion. Professor Richard Dawkins, in Lennonist manner, has suggested that the absence of religion would have allowed for the removal of many wars—from the Crusades, to Indian partition, to Israel-Palestine, to the former Yugoslavia, to Iraq, and beyond. The deployment of religious arguments in order to justify or legitimize war, and the idea that an historically active God is on your side in a conflict, have certainly persisted well into the modern period, and holy wars have possessed a variety of religious and denominational flavours. The Irish Civil War of the 1920s reflected a strongly held conviction by many that the cause of Irish republicans was deeply interwoven with Christian commitment. The IRA's Chief of Staff was clear in 1923, for example, about the nobility of an Irish Republican Army Volunteer 'offering his life and sufferings to God for the Republic of Ireland'.

But does such evidence necessarily suggest that Professor Dawkins's argument is correct, that religion is in itself a fundamental cause of war? One counter-argument is that religion is no more a fundamental cause for war than are other major human forces, and that human institutions and ideologies each have the capacity to be vehicles for or legitimators of violent conflict. Are churches, religious leaders, or politicians who use religious argument any more guilty of utilizing ideology for violent purpose than others (leaders of secular political parties, or secular people deploying arguments about democracy or human rights or justice or freedom)? Moreover, it should also be stressed that opponents of war have themselves often drawn on religious teachings, traditions, and beliefs.

A more subtle counter-argument seems to me to have even greater force, and it concerns the difficulty of mechanically separating out major religions from other elements of human society, in such a way as to suggest that if one removed 'religion', then this would have the kind of eirenic effect anticipated by Professor Dawkins. Any serious understanding of durable religions must be based on a recognition that, of necessity, these religions are simultaneously social and political as well as theological forces. Indeed, the idea of a major religion which is not intimately and influentially interwoven with questions of power, identity, economy, and authority within wider society, is one which could only be subscribed to by those who do not understand religion. It might well be that religious belief gives impetus towards some conflicts erupting, and some definition of them once they have done so, and this is an important enough claim to make (though it is worth here noting how often this involves rival forces using exactly the same texts and sources to justify opposing causes, which should caution against too mechanical a reading of supposedly religious causation).

Some have argued that a religious cause, with its numinous transcendence, allows for a more intense commitment, exhilaration, and apotheosis than do secular forces, thereby making bellicosity more likely. I am not persuaded that this is the case (when religion is compared, for instance, with extraordinarily heady quasi-religions such as nationalism). It seems to me that religious belief can contribute powerfully to arguments for war, interwoven with other (secular) impulses, without which the religious causation would be utterly insufficient; as Alan Wolfe has put it, 'Political religion is always two-faced, as much a force for such earthly goals as national solidarity or anti-colonial resistance as it is preoccupied with piety and purity'.

Those earthly goals often fall within the realm of economics, and economic impulsion—at group and also at individual level—towards an engagement in war has often been very strong. Although it is nowhere near as simple as that the 'have-nots' engage in warfare in order to grasp from the 'haves', states pursuing economic dominance, and individuals seeking direct economic advantage, have alike been drawn towards conflict partly for these reasons. For some who have engaged in modern war, such desire for economic, material benefit has clearly been a very important and even decisive motivation. At times, indeed, war has offered a chance for people to legitimate what would in other circumstances be seen more straightforwardly as self-serving crime.

The preceding argument of this chapter has reflected how far *Modern War* reaches beyond military history as such, and how strongly major societal and political forces are interwoven with one another when considered in relation to the causation of war. What causes modern wars to begin? No single pattern, but rather five key elements, have been considered. The nationalist politics of community, struggle, and power have provided momentum towards, capacity for, and justification of the starting of wars. Pursuit of sovereign statehood, and defence of it against various threats, have between them occasioned many conflicts; organized relationships between states have propelled them towards modern wars on occasion; and the failure of ordered states has also played its part in generating bloodshed. Imperial rivalry, and the establishment and aggrandisement and defence of empires, have likewise prompted conflict. Religious commitment has provided certainties which have contributed towards warfare, and has offered powerful rationalizations for it too. And economic imperative has, at various levels, generated conflict.

In much of this, the high-sounding, ostensible reasons offered by protagonists in explanation of war can be seen only partially to match the reality of causation, something evident when we consider how such multi-levelled multi-causation has worked in detailed historical practice.

So in what ways did the eruption of the First World War illustrate the themes set out above? When Bosnian-Serb teenager Gavrilo Princip killed Archduke Franz Ferdinand (heir to the Habsburg throne of Austria-Hungary) and his wife Sophie during their visit to Sarajevo on 28 June 1914, there could already be heard echoes of our complex causal framework. Princip was a member of Mlada Bosna (Young Bosnia), a nationalist-terrorist group which crossed religious divisions (Muslim, Catholic, Orthodox) and which was united instead by opposition to Austrian rule and by a desire for pan-Yugoslav unity. Behind them, Serbia (in turn backed by its protector, Russia) had been supportive of such nationalistic, terroristic, anti-Habsburg groups in Bosnia-Herzegovina; for its part, Austria-Hungary was not willing to let the Serbs eat away at their empire because, if the trend were not stemmed now, then worse would follow and disintegration ensue if the Slavs were allowed to enjoy impunity.

So nationalistic commitment, hostility to empire, contingent international alliances between states, and a desire to thwart rebellious violence early in its cycle, all appear already in this non-inevitable tale (as so often, a tale in which it is state response to terrorism, rather than terrorist violence itself, which most decisively changes history).

Following the Sarajevo assassinations, Germany backed Austria in taking a very harsh line with Serbia for its terrorist sponsorship, and in July 1914 the Austrians delivered a demanding ultimatum to Serbia; Serbia rejected it, and Austria declared war 28 July. Then state military mechanisms and commitments took over. On 30 July Tsar Nicholas mobilized all Russian troops (Russia backing and defending Serbia, a fellow Slavic state for which it acted as patron). On 1 August the mobilization order was given in Berlin, war being declared on Russia; German troops crossed into Belgium on 3 August, with Germany declaring war on France on the same day. The UK did not want the Low Countries to be in enemy hands (fearing dangerous, rivalrous threats to its own power and security and interests), and issued an ultimatum demanding assurances that Belgian neutrality be respected. These having been ignored, Britain declared war on 4 August 1914. So a series of (hierarchical) inter-state relations, a set of state imperatives and fears and ambitions, and a nationalistic set of commitments, played part of the decisive role in expanding Balkan antagonisms into cataclysmic world war.

None of this seems to me to have been inevitable. The pre-war arms race maybe made the conflict more likely, but arms races do not necessarily lead to conflicts. More specifically, Austria-Hungary's ultimatum to Serbia on 23 July stated that the Serbs had tolerated subversive groups against the Dual Monarchy and it demanded acknowledgement of Serb involvement, as well as calling for a set of other concessions including the dissolution of anti-Habsburg secret societies. This ultimatum was deliberately pitched so that it could not be agreed to, thereby offering a pretext for Austria-Hungary's declaration of war. The Serbs in fact agreed to most of the demands which had been made, but not to all of them, and the support of Russia for Serbia, and of Germany for Austria-Hungary, made a vital difference to that central, dyadic antagonism.

Thus a local flame burned into a world conflict between the Central Powers (Germany, Austria-Hungary) and the Entente Powers (Britain, France, Russia), with Bulgaria and Turkey entering the war on the side of the former, and Serbia, Belgium, Portugal, Rumania, Greece and—eventually—Italy and the USA siding with the latter.

Closer inspection of state motivation clarifies further the causal pattern which we have discussed. Germany (not least the insecure, deeply ambitious Kaiser Wilhelm II) wanted to be a world power, possessing a strong sense that it might have to go to war in order to achieve this hegemonic status; the Germans also felt relatively weak and vulnerable (losing the arms and naval races), and therefore saw the attractions of a pre-emptively ignited war, before their position became yet weaker: 1914 might be a more propitious moment to fight France and Russia than would a later date. By strongly supporting Austria-Hungary, the Germans knew that they were risking a war; but it was a war which they thought they would win. Encircled, trapped by the Triple Entente of France, Russia, and Britain, this powerful state saw war as a means towards securing, defending, and extending national power decisively.

Britain brought with it a competitive hegemonic ambition in relation to Germany, and saw real danger in the Germans defeating France and Russia and achieving greater relative power as a consequence. Recognizing German ambition towards grand imperial status as a world power, and the possibility of German control of western Europe if the Russians and French were defeated, Britain aimed to sustain its own position as the foremost, wealthiest nation in the world.

This is not to dismiss the justifications which were offered on different terms. Some in Britain did genuinely see a fight between Prussian militarism and democratic freedom as self-legitimating. And the Belgian pretext was not entirely empty. True, both Germany and Britain had been signatories to an 1839 Treaty guaranteeing Belgian neutrality; and Irish nationalist voices could legitimately protest that British concern for the rights and freedoms of small nations was somewhat illusory when it suited London for it to be so. But when the Germans invaded Belgium in 1914, though their atrocities were certainly on occasions exaggerated for propagandistic effect, this was the exaggeration of a practice of atrocity which did have a strong basis in fact. The German army *did* behave brutally towards many Belgian civilians, killing well over 5,000 during their march through the country, and destroying villages and towns as they proceeded.

Yet, despite the serious claim of defending Belgian neutrality, the central British aim was to prevent German aggrandisement and rivalry, and to protect the long-term security of Britain's empire. Moreover, as Avner Offer has pointed out, the fact that so much of British economic life did take an overseas, imperial form, had necessitated a strong navy, and had therefore accentuated fears of rivalry from Germany in this regard; so this had heightened the likelihood of British military action in response to German self-aggrandisement. In this sense, empire did indirectly help lead Britain to war in 1914.

French motivation for going to war was substantially defensive, against a genuine German threat and a longstanding German enemy. France could not allow Russia to lose in war to Germany without thereby facilitating German hegemony over Europe. Bound by treaty to help Russia in such circumstances anyway, the French priority was to ensure that Germany was not able to dominate Europe, and additional benefits (such as regaining Alsace and Lorraine) reinforced this impulsion.

For its part, Russia possessed a huge empire, with a population of some 164 million in 1914, and with associated needs for prestige maintenance in international relations. The Russians could not really abandon Serbia to being humiliatingly crushed by Austria-Hungary, without abandoning the Slav cause (with which they felt a strong affinity, and for which they acted as protector). So claims that they were fighting for the interests of their fellow Slavs, and to defend their ally, France, were not entirely false.

Austria-Hungary could legitimately claim that, in going to war, it was protecting its historic empire from disintegration (a disintegration favoured by its old adversary, Russia). There was an understandable anxiety that, if nothing was done about Balkan nationalism and pan-Slavism, then imperial dismantling might follow.

To be sure, original motivations could become overwhelmed and amended as the dynamics of the war sped forward, and most had anticipated a shorter conflict than was bloodily to emerge in fact. But we do have here a complex set of historical circumstances which offer detailed echoes of our pattern of war's historical creation, as rivalry between intensely nationalistic states and rivalrous empires saw them jolt towards war, desirous of protecting economic and sovereign interests and rights and to prevent the expansion of competitors' power.

Within all this, the contingent role of the individual could be crucial, as in later conflicts. The cascade towards the Second World War would have been utterly different (perhaps impossible) without the part played by Adolf Hitler; but less world-dominating figures also reflected the vital role of the contingently personal, the idiosyncratic, and therefore the jagged, messy, and unpredictably complex. Mussolini's 1937 assertion (quoted by Simon Ball) that England was 'a nation which thinks with its arse' neatly exemplifies the personalized angles from which decisive leaders can sometimes view war-related matters, just as his capricious inconsistency and pathetic tendency towards pursuit of the heroic further complicated patterns of bellicose behaviour in this period.

There has been a trend in recent decades away from inter-state war: as Kalyvas has pointed out, of the 118 armed conflicts between 1989 and 2004, only seven have been inter-state; and (as Jeremy Weinstein has recorded) during the 1990s, over 90 per cent of deaths in war took place in internal, rather than inter-state, conflicts. But the broad pattern we have discussed for the 1914 case remains pertinent, I think, despite this. The 1991 Gulf War saw a quasi-imperial power (the United States of America) decide that an economically important region of the world required the halting of the aggrandisement of an antagonistic state (Saddam Hussein's Iraq), over the infringement of national sovereignty (with Hussein's August 1990 invasion of Kuwait), and the protection of an oil-rich ally (Saudi Arabia) in the process.

Through all this, does the (now fashionable again) idea of human nature offer hermeneutical help? Is there, to be blunt, something in our nature as humans which causes, and explains the causes of, war? Recourse to evil itself does not really help, since it is hard to reconcile either the notion of a pervasive human instinct for evil, or an inherent human goodness, with the extraordinary variety of individual and group actions over time and across place in relation to violence. Put starkly, if human nature is so elastic as to allow for so many variations in our responses and decisions about war, then its explanatory power seems attenuated as a result.

It remains hard not to categorize, for example, Nazi war-time brutality as evil. But does describing something as 'evil' help us any better to understand and explain why so many normal people did such abnormally awful things? Professor Alan Wolfe's emphasis on 'political' evil is valuable here, I think. Wolfe defines 'political evil' as 'the wilful, malevolent, and gratuitous death, destruction, and suffering inflicted upon innocent people by the leaders of movements and states in their strategic efforts to achieve realizable objectives', and he identifies four contemporary species of political evil: 'terrorism, ethnic cleansing, genocide, and a reliance on means such as torture to fight back against evil'. All four can be considered relevant to modern war, and Wolfe's argument is subtle, precise, and thoughtful. He argues (regarding human nature) that we need a 'moralistic realism': unrealistic goals are of little value, but state policies—in terms of their foreign dealings, for example—require a moral dimension. According to this view, a combination of morality and practical, honest realism is what is needed in responding to the evil elements of human politics, in war as in other areas of endeavour.

* * *

'Well, what are *you* going to the war for?' asked Pierre.

'What for? I don't know. Because I have to. Besides, I am going…' He stopped. 'I am going because the life I lead here—is not to my taste!'

Leo Tolstoy, *War and Peace*, vol. i (1865)

Born in 1828, writing in the 1860s, and dying before the First World War had inaugurated 20th-century catastrophic warfare, Tolstoy—himself a soldier—here captures something of the uncertain complexity of individual combatant motivation. It might comfort states to maintain that their soldiers' war-time motives have neatly matched the ostensible reasons given by the state itself for having gone to war. The historical reality has repeatedly been, however, that states' given reasons for fighting wars represent only partially adequate explanations for their soldiers' actual engagement in those brutal conflicts. This is not to deny the frequent effectiveness of ideologies and institutions in operationalizing and sustaining individual participation, by making it seem natural, just, appropriate, necessary, or even inevitable for the individual to take part in warfare. We have seen the role of nationalism here already; and discursive and institutional continuities do indeed often help to reproduce war again and again. But to explain why states go to war, and why soldiers actually take part in warfare, is to explain two different (albeit partly overlapping) phenomena.

The explanation for people fighting turns out to comprise a many-layered set of processes and decisions and impulses, involving the rational, the visceral, the coercive, and the habitual all contributing variously to our blood-spattered phenomenon. People may indeed have several reasons and motivations towards fighting and then continuing to fight, and it might be helpful to disaggregate them here into the ostensible, the individually instrumental, and the emotional.

Ostensible explanations involve the reasons given for the commencement of the war in question, whether the defence of national freedom, the pursuit of other ideological goals, the righting of wrongs against a particular community, or whatever. However sceptical one might be about state or national or communal justifications for war-time violence, there is no doubt that, for example, nationalism and allegiance to national rights and freedoms have indeed played their part in motivating people to fight and die on occasion in practice. I myself doubt that ideological motivation runs as deep as war-time speeches and propaganda, or post-war commemoration, often tend to imply. But soldiers *are* sometimes ideologically motivated, and people do on occasions actually fight for their beliefs. Though the UK popular response was complex, there was not a shortage of initial zeal in Britain at the start of the First World War: more than a million men enlisted by the end of 1914; more than 2.2 million had enlisted by September the following year. On such a scale, the argument that enthusiasm was purely because one's friends joined up risks a certain circularity, and it seems unavoidable on the evidence to conclude that widespread nationalist commitment, and a strong desire to defend the nation, played a part in motivating individuals to enlist.

Nor does this rule out the simultaneous attraction offered by another layer of motivation: the individually instrumental. People's involvement in military forces and their bellicose activities once in them can be prompted alike by a need or desire for a job, money, career opportunities of various kinds, the allure of professionalism as such, and also the possibility of prestige, social or sexual advantage, and the direct acquisition of goods during wartime. Economic necessity and social goods can be as important as fighting to defend your nation (as Adrian Gregory has put it, 'Economic distress had always been the British Army's best recruiting agent'). Likewise, another form of necessity can come into play: if people are conscripted, and then coerced into fighting once in uniform, then the space for choice about whether to fight can be very restricted and has been so historically on many occasions in the modern era. The January 1916 British Military Service Act conscripted all single men between eighteen and forty-one years of age: in such circumstances, the costs of not fighting might seem to outweigh the benefits. So the banal issues of salaries and vanity and greed and unavoidable obedience play their part.

So too do the emotions in other ways again, and while it is hard to segregate the instrumental from the visceral, it is worth stressing that excitement, adventure, and personal loyalty often seem important in making people decide to fight. There is now a strong scholarly basis for believing that small-group intimacy of attachment, solidarity, and mutual loyalty plays at least as large a role in motivating soldiers actually to fight (and to keep on fighting) as does a larger-framed factor such as nationalist ideology; First World War 'Pals' battalions provided a frequently poignant example and—as hinted already—it is often the actual rather than the imagined community which jolts people into fighting and dying. One's friends, local community, and local loyalties can be the decisive elements here, as can honour, pride, a desire for glory, comradeship, solidarity, a zeal to protect the precious, and also a vengeful, hate-filled striking back at enemies once the game is afoot. The contingently relational matters here, as the perceived or historical actions of one's enemies generate reaction in an antiphonal sequence, defining and driving people's war-time acts as they do so; war can possess a self-sustaining dynamic, once begun. As Paul Preston has brilliantly demonstrated, during the 1936–9 Spanish Civil War prior enmities, but also a desire to avenge enemy actions which had been carried out during the war itself, both played their part in stimulating combatants actually to fight.

It would be naïve to assume uniform commitment to fighting, even once the guns have started firing. Some oppose the fight, while others quietly go along with it, doing the minimum, being opportunistic, and not putting their shoulder forcefully to the war-machine wheel. And, for those who do engage sincerely, there can exist layered, multiple, simultaneous motivations even at the individual level—so much so that those not involved can have a sense of missing out on what is central, as fictionally depicted here in relation to the Second World War, and Philip Roth's ineligible Bucky Cantor: 'Time and again it seemed as if everybody had gone off to war except him. To have been preserved from the fighting, to have escaped the bloodshed—all that someone else might have considered a boon, he saw as an affliction. He was raised to be a fearless battler by his grandfather, trained to think he must be a hugely responsible man, ready and fit to defend what was right, and instead, confronted with the struggle of the century, a worldwide conflict between good and evil, he could not take even the smallest part'.

The reasons for people's commitment are always context-specific. Why did people actually fight in the Vietnam War? Most Western attention has focused on the US forces, but motivation for enlisting and fighting in the National Liberation Front (NLF)/Viet Cong (VC) is equally revealing, and depends also on a reading of local nuance. It does not seem that people joined primarily because of an ideological commitment to communism. As Tovy has pointed out, the peasants who joined up seem more to have been motivated by a combination of family loyalty (following family members into the NLF/VC), by a desire to improve their economic situation and standard of living, by the pursuit of revenge for prior violence (by the French, the South Vietnamese government, or the United States), by the appeal of Vietnamese unificatory nationalism, and also by the straightforward appeal of adventure. That the Communists offered the presumed best route towards these goals meant that the ideological and these other impulses were overlain, interwoven. But, just as with the multiple reasons for young Americans to fight against them, the NLF/VC carried mixed rationalizations for their own violent engagement.

Causation

* * *

In human behaviour few events are more difficult to predict than the course and duration of a war

Geoffrey Blainey, *The Causes of War*

Having reflected on why modern wars begin, and on why people fight in them once they have started, let's now turn to the question of why they have ended. Sheer victory offers combatants the most alluring reason, whether on the basis of decisive battles and superior tactics; or of brilliant and charismatic leadership, better preparedness, or greater psychological resolve; or of overwhelming superiority in terms of numbers of people, technological sophistication, firepower, discipline, morale, and economic resources. Clearly, these elements can combine. The 1861–5 American Civil War saw the technological, numerical, and industrial superiority of the North eventually win out against the South; but psychology also played a part, as the latter had less will than did their opponents for the prospect of a long war of appalling attrition. The 1870–1 Franco-Prussian War saw the Prussians mobilize far more rapidly than the French, and this faster mobility did facilitate victory—but so also did better, prior Prussian training, and in May 1871 France had to agree to the humiliating terms of the Treaty of Frankfurt as a consequence.

Yet wars frequently end far more messily and much less crisply than this, and superior technology is not necessarily the decisive element in determining their duration. War's conclusion often emerges very blurredly, with a far from smooth shift from war to peace. Not only do some military fronts drag on while others reach a conclusion, but it can be difficult even after war has ended to achieve full peace anyway, as the latter can remain compromised by painful remnants of war. One often finds, historically, a kind of low-grade and deeply flawed peace, within which lie the seeds for potential, future warfare. Post-war peace is rarely promptly absolute.

Stalemate-induced, compromise endings can be relevant here, as is the issue of what happens to former combatants. Where there have been determined efforts to reintegrate former fighters, then some success (messy and unsatisfactory though it tends to be) can prove possible—the case of former KLA (Kosovo Liberation Army) members in Kosovo perhaps providing an example. But relationships tend, understandably, not to have been healed, attitudes towards former enemies remaining unaltered or worsened by conflict, with what preceded the violence living on sullenly after its conclusion. So, as Shirlow et al. have shown, the long, late-20th-century war in Northern Ireland ended without those who had been involved in violent groups on rival sides tending to change their fundamentally hostile readings of former adversaries from the opposing community.

What of patterns evident from even more serious conflicts than the late-20th-century Ulster crisis? At 11am on 11 November 1918 the First World War formally ended, the Paris Peace Conference then beginning on 18 January 1919, and resulting in the triumphant but flawed Treaty of Versailles. In part, Allied victory followed a successful spring 1918 campaign, in which the weight of forces during March–June proved decisive (France, Britain, the USA, Portugal, Belgium, and Italy all being involved). Here, the scale of men and economic power available to the Allies ultimately drowned the Central Powers. So, despite the Germans arguably having been more efficient in mobilizing and fighting with their resources, they were defeated partly for the huge and simple reason of the scale of the resources set against them. But contingency, rather than sheer inevitability, played its part in this process: ill-judged German provocation brought the USA into the conflict (the latter declaring war on 5 April 1917), and the injection of new resources thus made available was staggering. By the start of 1918 there were a million US troops in France, and in 1918 itself American troops were arriving in France at the rate of 150,000 per month. The boost here to resources, but also to morale, was deeply significant and near-overwhelming. For the Germans, years of suffering, shortages of food, mutiny in the armed forces, and domestic strikes, between them sapped the strength of the cause, and reserves of troops were exhausted by 1918.

When the Second World War ended on 14 August 1945 there had again been an issue of overwhelming numbers and resources, with the USA and USSR helping to drown the German opposition. The Allies enjoyed far larger reservoirs of resources, economically and militarily, than did the Axis powers; ultimately, Germany was defeated when militarily bashed into submitting, when economically devastated, and when occupied brutally by its adversaries.

But leadership too had played its part, Churchillian charisma being complemented by Hitlerian errors (spectacularly, in the case of invading the Soviet Union in 1941). Historians will tend to stress the importance of contingencies, even down to the role of an individual's ability, formation, decision-making, and career. It remains hard to see that Britain's Second World War success and even survival would have been quite as they were had Churchill not been quite who he was, with his very distinctive combination of boldness, ambition, inspiring eloquence, intuition, insight, and dominant dedication (Figure 5).

More broadly, three years of planning had gone into the D-Day landings of 6 June 1944, just as considerable bravery contributed to their success at the time. And—even as recorded in pacifist Frances Partridge's diary account, written from a largely quiescent and bohemian Wiltshire—it could be seen that the last stage of the War was 'shaping to some vast Wagnerian finale'. The Second World War in Europe officially ended on 8 May 1945 with German unconditional surrender to the Allies. The USA, the Soviet Union, the UK, and France took over formally in Germany with the Berlin Declaration of 5 June, and brutality marred this victory over evil. Regarding the Russians at this stage of Allied victory and the occupation of Germany, British commander Bernard 'Monty' Montgomery—himself far from squeamish, and someone who viewed life as 'a stern struggle'—was stark in the bleakness of his assessment:

> From their behaviour it soon became clear that the Russians, though a fine fighting race, were in fact barbarous Asiatics who had never enjoyed a civilization comparable to that of the rest of Europe. Their approach to every problem was utterly different from

5. Sir Winston Churchill, 1874–1965

ours and their behaviour, especially in their treatment of women, was abhorrent to us.

A bizarre German resilience was also evident at the end. Professor Ian Kershaw's brilliant monograph on the demise of Hitler's Germany in 1944–5 asks the troubling question of why, with defeat so obvious and imminent during those years, many Germans not only fought loyally on, but engaged in continued brutality against internal enemy groups. Holding out until May 1945 ensured the hideous destruction of Germany and its people (the losses in the Wehrmacht were running at 350,000 *per month* during the last period of the war), and this perseverative bellicosity is historically rare. Its causes were numerous, among them Hitler's own refusal to accept surrender or compromise, the crushing effect on opposition of the regime's own terroristic violence, the striking efficacy of certain players in Hitler's team (most notably, Albert Speer), and a genuine, pervasive fear of Bolshevism. But it also included the 'structures and mentalities' of the Nazi order, which sustained Hitler's personalized rule, power, and bureaucratically-upheld regime to the death.

Consideration of the ending of individual, major conflicts might prompt brief reflection on the issue of attempting an end to war itself, or at least attempting to provide for systematic prevention. An historian's instinctive, repeatedly reinforced scepticism makes it hard to resist Paul Hirst's pithy claim that, 'War has a future. There is no danger of universal and perpetual peace breaking out in this century'. In part, this reflects the central Hobbesian problem of the modern (and possibly of any) period, which can be set out in three inter-linked statements: first, people on various sides of a community claim as good or right what is, or seems to be, in their own sectional interest; second, they tend to argue that one opinion (their own) deserves widespread acceptance within the broad community because it is right and good and true; third, in reality, it is not the finally decisive victory of one opinion that we will be likely to witness, but rather the persistence of different, rival, and clashing interests. Our Hobbesian challenge is to devise effective means of preventing these rival interests and views from erupting into blood-spattered warfare.

Despite my fundamental pessimism, I am struck by how much progress has been made in constraining human viciousness, in war as beyond, and it is worth reflecting on this process and on those attempts people have made to strengthen such constraints. Steven Pinker's admirably ambitious attempt to explain why 'violence has declined over long stretches of time' and why 'today we may be living in the most peaceable era in our species' existence' centres on five historical forces which he argues to have increasingly produced peaceable behaviour, 'five developments that have pushed the world in a peaceful direction': the evolution of a state sustaining the Weberian monopoly on the legitimate use of force within its territory; mutually beneficial commerce and trade; the feminization of cultures, away from more aggressive male instincts; an expansion of cosmopolitanism allowing for greater empathy and sympathy with others; and an upward trend in the application of reason to our affairs. Much of Pinker's decline in violence (relative to population) relates to various kinds of war. Benignly, it is clear that major armed conflicts have diminished in number during the post-1989 period, while the popular view that civilians in war are worse off now than they were previously is almost certainly false.

In broad terms, there does seem then to have been some possibly eirenic value in establishing and sustaining states which enjoy effective control over their territory, as implied by the UK Ministry of Defence in its 2010 paper assessing future challenges, the *Future Character of Conflict*: 'State failure will be one of the dominant, defining features of future conflict.... States that cannot adapt to the changing global context will risk collapse, and many such failures will be accompanied by substantial outbreaks of violence.' Likewise, there has been great significance in producing mutually beneficial commerce, and in furthering cultural shifts towards the rational, empathetic, and humanely cosmopolitan, as we try to explain the fact that what Pinker calls 'war-free years' have been growing in number; systems of effective economic cooperation (and peaceful competition) have made war less attractive to many states; in the developed world mutually beneficial economic interdependence has made war much less alluring. Advanced states tend not to see economic rivalry between them as a cause for war (indeed, war would damage the stability of the market system from which most of them gain greatly).

If we are to avoid a sense of hopelessness, then reflection on that potentially catastrophic phenomenon—nuclear war—might paradoxically prove reasonably encouraging. William Walker's deeply thoughtful account of nuclear weapons has pointed out that, while the ongoing and awful threat of nuclear war lastingly endures, much has been achieved since the weapon's creation in the 1940s in terms of restraint in its use. The nuclear order has been Protean and at times fragile, crisis-laden, and confrontational. But nuclear weapons have not been deployed in warfare since 1945 and—given the terrible consequences of their use—this represents a huge achievement. The goal of ridding the world of nuclear weapons remains essentially quixotic. But what Walker himself calls a pragmatic 'logic of restraint' (regarding war, regarding the use of nuclear weapons *in* war, and regarding people's acquisition of nuclear weapons capacity) has provided a solid basis for avoiding disaster thus far. Part of this, of course, has involved comparative success in avoiding wars themselves between major states; and some of that avoidance seems clearly to have rested on the unthinkably annihilating horror of nuclear war, should conflict between nuclear-armed states actually develop. New challenges now will need to be met in a post-Cold War era of nuclear multi-polarity; but the centrality of states to nuclear bellicosity and threat—and the changing dynamics of inter-state, great-power relationships—will probably remain decisive, despite (probably exaggerated) fears of non-state terrorist nuclear violence.

There has, even now, been much less research on peace than there has on war, despite some impressive contributions. But the two phenomena—war and peace—are at times only blurrily separated in historical practice, and the interconnections between them are vital to our understanding of modern war. Even ostensibly peace-loving nations can have deeply bellicose histories: the United States of America has seen its military engaged in campaigns for over half of the years of the country's existence. And to pursue the eradication of war would be as naïve as to pursue human or moral perfection; the effective curtailment of particular wars, or specific war-time brutality, almost certainly depends instead on recognizing our appalling capacity for (and even our historical tendency towards) justifying and practising violent atrocity.

For the prospect of establishing human behaviour along lines guided too closely by idealized blueprints probably exaggerates human capacity for improvement. Amartya Sen's excellent, quasi-Burkean distinction between realization-focused comparison and transcendental institutionalism points one way forward in response. Professor Sen's dichotomy here is between: a focus on people's actual behaviour and influences, one which concentrates on removing or preventing egregious injustice; and an approach based on an identification of perfect justice, and the creation of institutions appropriate to such perfection. The former allows for making things (in our deeply imperfect context) relatively less awful, in arguably more achievable fashion; the latter risks hubris, counter-productive ambition, and often the time-wasting political engineering of supposedly just institutions.

Historians tend to be sceptical about the degree to which messily subversive human behaviour will comply in practice with even the most rationally and benevolently designed institutions and orders, and this rather urges one—as with Sen's argument—towards unsatisfactory but feasible improvement, rather than blueprint-led, arrangement-based efforts at perfectibility. Such scholars will look knowingly at the 1920–46 League of Nations period and its overwhelming ineffectiveness, or at the frequent inoperability of the 1949 Geneva Conventions on the protection of those victims of war who fall into enemy hands.

But even the harshest sceptic should note also that, while the United Nations since 1945 has been unable to prevent wars, the body has offered some basis for collective deliberation and action in crisis, and has at times limited states' recourse to warfare. Its record has been far from wonderful in terms of preventing either inter- or intra-state conflicts, but it has prevented *some*; and it has also done much work—despite many enduring obstacles—to protect civilian populations from war's worst effects. Moreover, there has been a substantial number of international agreements, during the past fifty years, to limit the proliferation and use of weapons, and the effect of these in minimizing awfulness should not be casually dismissed.

In truth, at present, only the United States is in a position realistically to attempt to enforce peace, and the line here between internationally imposed peace and neo-imperialism is not always easy to draw very firmly or clearly. It remains hard to see such interventions as purely humanitarian or altruistic, however beneficial they may be judged by dispassionate observers; it remains equally difficult to identify any other effective actor capable of enforcing peace in political practice.

Traditional wars fought about sovereignty and territory probably still have some life in them yet, with the contingencies of power elites and even of ruling individuals playing a role which would not have been unrecognizable to observers from previous generations of warfare. States have continued to fight each other in recent decades, and although much attention has rightly been focused on civil wars, these are far from being the only kind of major threat of violent conflict which we face and will continue to face.

Yet it is possible to sense a more restricted kind of war in coming decades too. As General Sir Peter Wall, Chief of the UK General Staff, pointed out in 2012, the United Kingdom's plans for its Army in 2020 involve a centrally three-fold purpose (conventional intervention/deterrence, overseas involvement in multinational efforts to prevent conflict from erupting, and domestic preparedness for eventualities such as floods), only one part of which focuses on orthodox war. Attempting to abolish war remains jejune and quixotic; limiting its likelihood remains, on a case by case basis, far more plausible. 'Less violence' might seem a rather weaker ambition that 'non-violence', but it is probably more valuably realistic given the complex causation and likelihood of continuing threats of war.

Hannah Arendt, writing in the summer of 1950, argued that, 'Two World Wars in one generation, separated by an uninterrupted chain of local wars and revolutions, followed by no peace treaty for the vanquished and no respite for the victor, have ended in the anticipation of a third World War between the two remaining world powers'. In fact, that anticipated War turned out to be Cold, and far more peaceful. On the same broad topic, but I think with greater acuity of vision than even the great Arendt, Alan Wolfe has sagely pointed out that, 'When confronted with political evil, we are better off responding to the "political" rather than to the "evil"'. Focusing on the political and the historical—and examining honestly the real, local causes and dynamics—allows for minimizing (perhaps) some specific threats to peace; 'recognizing that evil can have a political character reminds us that politics is, and always will be, the best means of dealing with it'.

Chapter 3
Lived experience

'They're trying to kill me,' Yossarian told him calmly.
'No one's trying to kill you,' Clevinger cried.
'Then why are they shooting at me?' Yossarian asked.
'They're shooting at *everyone*,' Clevinger answered. 'They're trying to kill everyone.'
'And what difference does that make?'

Joseph Heller, *Catch-22* (1961)

The outrageous cynicism of Joseph Heller's famous novel of Second World War absurdity remains distressingly pungent more than five decades after its publication. Milo Minderbinder's economic opportunism in profit-making from the conflict, from his comrades, and from their suffering, is familiar to anyone intimate with the details of having a good commercial war in the 21st century: 'Look, I didn't start this war...I'm just trying to put it on a businesslike basis. Is anything wrong with that?' The apparently unjust insanity of so many rules and authorities encasing war and its warriors is repeatedly evoked throughout the novel: 'Colonel Korn was the lawyer, and if Colonel Korn assured him that fraud, extortion, currency manipulation, embezzlement, income tax evasion, and black market speculations were legal, Colonel Cathcart was in no position to disagree with him'. And without 'the handy technique of protective rationalization', few war leaders, soldiers, or armies would find it possible to live with conflict as well as they have done throughout so much of modern history.

Of course, matters remain far more complex and (as McLoughlin has shown) war is enduringly difficult to depict, whether due to its scale or its chaotic and extreme character. In this chapter I want briefly to consider the heterogeneous nature of the experience of war, and to do so under four headings: horror, boredom, exhilaration, and opportunity. This involves a necessary simplification, since people's experience of war will vary so greatly according to the background and assumptions of the person concerned, and the cultural and historical location against which they are undergoing the experience. Geography, social class, gender, age, profession, and historical period between them mean that there can be no uniform accounting for the experience of modern war.

But the place to start has to be with the horror—indeed, the profound terror—of so much of the experience of modern war, and to do so through authoritatively first-hand accounts. This is not always popular. In the words of one long-time, expert observer of war-plagued zones (the journalist, Peter Beaumont), 'it is still regarded as bad form to describe the reality of the everyday horror of conflict. But to understand conflict one must confront what people do when they kill and mutilate'. For it could be argued that the central truth about modern war is its awful, baneful, devastating, and horrific brutality. Much of this also involves extra-combat atrocity such as rape (as in the wars occasioned by Indian partition, or during the defeat of Germany in 1944–5), or torture and extra-judicial murder during war-time (as in the 1930s Spanish Civil War).

The First World War remains perhaps the most tragically vivid illustration of war-related, annihilating horror and, though well-known, its terrifying details deserve explicit statement.

Wilfred Owen's famous poem *Dulce Et Decorum Est* horribly reminds us that chemical warfare has a long history (around a million troops were probably wounded by chemical weapons during the 1914–18 War): 'Gas! GAS!... the white eyes writhing in his face... If you could hear, at every jolt, the blood/Come gargling from the froth-corrupted lungs'. And gas, first deployed by the Germans in 1915, was soon widely used by both sides; results included horrifying burns, serious lung damage, and death by asphyxiation. H. G. Wells's First World War novel, *Mr Britling Sees It Through* (published in 1916), contemporaneously and rightly identified the undoubted 'malignity of warfare', 'the immediate horror of war, the dense cruel stupidity of the business, plain and close'.

Some aspects of the Great War's experience were effectively unbearable for those who went through them, with a haunting, normality-eroding memory long outliving the wretched conflict itself. Wide-angled reflections and statistics rather validate such responses. As Robson has pointed out, of the 410,000 British/Commonwealth soldiers at Gallipoli in 1915, 205,000 were left killed, wounded, sick, or missing after the encounter. By the spring of 1915 the Austrian army had lost around two million men; for its part, by the end of 1915 the Russian army had lost in the region of four million. By the end of the 1916 battle of the Somme alone, the Allies had lost around 600,000 men, with only tragically minor achievement to show for it; on 1 July 1916 itself, 993 British Army officers and 18,247 from other ranks died in that appalling battle. Not for nothing did the Somme come to be known among British troops as the Great Fuck-Up. Passchendaele—31 July until 12 November 1917—saw German losses of about 200,000 during four months of repeated horror. As Niall Ferguson reminds us, of 557,618 Scots who enlisted in the British Army during the First World War, 26.4 per cent died. John Buchan—himself a Scot—piercingly noted of the War, 'Losses, which a few years before would have seemed cataclysmal, became a matter of course'. And the effect on the killers could be stark at times also, as is captured in a letter from T. E. Lawrence in September 1917:

> I hope when the nightmare ends that I will wake up and become alive again. This killing and killing of Turks is horrible. When you charge in at the finish and find them all over the place in bits, and still alive many of them, and know that you have done hundreds in the same way before and must do hundreds more if you can.

For the War as a whole, the figures remain even more shocking. Not only was the scale of military involvement remarkable (five and a quarter million men served in the British Army during 1914–18, for example); the resultant tallies of dead and injured were monumental, whichever sources and estimates one deploys. Michael Howard records the War dead as follows: Central Powers—Austria-Hungary 1,200,000, Germany 1,800,000, Turkey 320,000, Bulgaria 90,000; Allied Powers—France 1,400,000, Britain 740,000, British Empire 170,000, Russia 1,700,000, Italy 460,000, USA 115,000. Ferguson offers the following estimates of War casualties: total Allied deaths 5,421,000, total Allied wounded 7,025,487; total Central Powers deaths 4,029,000; total Central Powers wounded 8,379,418. In the Second World War, according to Max Hastings, an average of 27,000 people died *each day* during the September 1939–August 1945 period as a result of the conflict.

This horrific viciousness of war could prompt understandable fear, although across many conflicts the latter often seems to have been sharper in anticipation than it was in the midst of conflict. A British marine—quoted in Charles Townshend's invaluable edited volume on modern war, and looking back at the Falklands War—suggested that: 'people were frightened before it began rather than while it was going on'. Fear and panic could also involve those suffering from war as non-combatants, whether bereaved, injured, threatened, or forced to endure refugee status.

Indeed, the deliberate targeting of civilians has formed a major aspect of the experience of modern war. Regarding the Royal Air Force's Second World War bombing of Germany, the Commander of RAF Bomber Command (Sir Arthur Harris) favoured area-bombing—namely, the attacking of German cities—which effectively maximized the chances of hitting industrial targets, but also of causing significant civilian casualties and mass terror. Huge numbers of people were killed and maimed in such terrifying assaults. During July and August 1943 the RAF and US Army Air Force bombed and substantially destroyed the German city of Hamburg, with over 50,000 people being killed. Such was their power, the flames became a firestorm, with people—many of them civilians—being ineluctably sucked into the fires and killed. In the apt words of Michael Howard (who had joined the British Army the previous year), 'war was a thoroughly Bad Thing'. German V-1 and V-2 rockets had also targeted London from 1944—rocket-propelled flying bombs that arrived without warning (Figures 6 and 7).

But these terrifying experiences of the horror of war vary greatly, not only between but also within conflicts. Why are levels of terrible violence so divergent across and within modern wars?

Let's examine two very impressive recent scholarly attempts at solving part of this problem. Tim Wilson's brilliant analysis of early 20th-century national self-determination conflicts in Ulster and Upper Silesia suggests the importance of the nature of the boundary which divides different ethnic or national groups from one another during a war. He argues that the much higher levels and more gruesome types of violence in 1918–22 Upper Silesia (as compared with contemporary Ulster) can best be explained on this basis. In Ulster, religion provided the communal line of division and it did so in a solid, clear way: one was clearly and unmistakably either Catholic or Protestant. By contrast, Upper Silesia was overwhelmingly united in religion, and its people were

6. Damage done by German rockets in London, 1944

7. Damage done by Allied bombing, Hamburg, 1943

divided by the much more ambiguous fact of language (German or Polish). Religion functioned 'as a "hard" dividing line between rival communities in Ulster. Language in Upper Silesia acted in a very different fashion—as a "soft" (that is, permeable) boundary between national camps.' For people could speak more than one language, and the dialect of one language might involve modification into hybridity by contact with another; language therefore represented a far less certain marker of different nationality and of separateness than did the more solid line of religious attachment in Ulster.

Wilson's argument here is that Ulster's more clear-cut religious boundary required less (and less intense and grotesque) violence to maintain it, than was needed to establish communal difference in Upper Silesia, where division was marked by the more fluid, porous, and unstable line of linguistic division. In Ulster, 'where boundaries were already so clear between unionists and nationalists, less violence was needed to maintain division'. The limited task of Ulster boundary maintenance could afford to be less transgressive and bloody than the more ambitious Upper Silesian process of boundary creation: 'In short: atrocity clarified allegiances', and 'not all identity boundaries function the same way in national conflicts'.

An equally brilliant, very different argument regarding variations in levels and types of violence has been offered by Jeremy Weinstein, who suggests that the explanation for some insurgent groups acting abusively, brutally, and violently in conflict with civilian populations, while others engage more harmoniously and consensually with them, lies in the initial conditions of group formation, and especially in the varied endowments and resources available to such groups when they mobilize. According to Weinstein, groups with easy access to material resources tend to attract low-commitment, opportunistic 'consumers' as members—effectively, people keen on short-term gain. Rebel groups which, by contrast, have no such easy access to material or economic resources, draw in more committed, long-termist 'investors' as recruits; they rely on more harmonious engagement with communities, drawing on social resources and connections (shared ethnicity, shared religion) for sustenance; and they deploy violence more restrainedly, discriminatingly, and selectively as a result. The former are less disciplined and more coercive; the latter, more cooperative, and less prone to extreme violence and to self-serving plunder. Although perhaps vulnerable to charges of over-simplifying rebel identities (are people really so neatly classifiable as *either* investors *or* consumers?) and of attributing behaviour too narrowly to rationality alone ('I begin with the assumption that individuals are rational and that their actions reflect deliberate decisions designed to maximize payoffs'), this extremely well-researched, closely focused, comparative argument about political violence powerfully leads us away from an over-concentration on rhetorical self-justifications, and towards a valuable layer of interpretation and explanation for varied strategies and tactics adopted in war (in this case, in civil wars).

Whether or not one is persuaded by their arguments, what Wilson and Weinstein both powerfully articulate is a case for establishing what the key variables actually are when we try to account for greater (or lesser) levels of atrocious violence in war. Moreover, they do this by testing wide-angled arguments and hypotheses valuably against detailed, first-hand knowledge of particular violent contexts.

First-hand evidence can provide nuanced understanding of exactly how individuals themselves calibrated and dealt with their pain. Charles Rodger Walker, born in Montrose in Scotland, served in the British forces in Palestine during 1917–19 (Figure 8). Writing in September 1918 to his mother, he recounted his latest injury, phlegmatically and with a sense of proportion and real pride in success against the enemy:

8. Charles Rodger Walker, who served in the British forces in Palestine, 1917–19

Dear Mother,

I have been wounded a second time. At 4.30 am on the morning of the 19th we were lying out in 'No Man's Land' with the infantry about to begin the great attack which you must have heard of by now. I was just in the act of getting to my feet when I felt as if a clod of earth hit me a great whack on the right shoulder. Not feeling any blood, I thought this had really been the cause and I advanced with the others. After we had come through Johnny's barrage and had reached our first objective, the excitement having died down a bit, I made investigations and discovered that a rifle bullet had penetrated my shoulder.... Luckily it did not go very deep and I had it successfully extracted this forenoon ... The wound, of course, is more severe than the last which was a mere scratch, but the pain has now greatly lessened, and you need not let the news alarm you.... Well, we have got the old Turk properly on the hop this time, and prisoners come in thick and fast.

(Charles Rodger Walker to his Mother, 21 September 1918, University of St Andrews Library, Department of Special Collections, Ms 38096/15)

And if modern war can be terrorizing, horrific, and painful, it can also be very dull. John Buchan, someone whose view and representation of war are often seen as over-celebratory and rather romanticized, also looked back at the First World War with the reflection that he had 'acquired a bitter detestation of war, less for its horrors than for its boredom and futility'. Nearly a century later, one embedded journalist (Sebastian Junger) referred to US soldiers in Afghanistan in terms of a 'boredom so relentless that the men openly hope for an attack'. The distinguished military historian Michael Howard—who lost many friends to war—delightfully suggested that war, like cricket, consists 'of nine parts boredom to one part terror'. As Clausewitz recognized, inaction formed a large part of the actual experience of war: 'standing still and doing nothing is quite plainly the normal condition of an army in the midst of war, acting, the exception'; this reality remained true even in conflicts as significant and sustained as the Second World War, during which many soldiers did not actually fire their guns. For the broader point must be acknowledged that, much of the time in modern war, soldiers do not fight, and indeed choose *not* to try to kill their enemies. Indeed, war experience can be deeply inconsequential. As Eric Hobsbawm observed:

> The best way of summing up my personal experience of the Second World War is to say that it took six and a half years out of my life, six of them in the British army. I had neither a 'good war' nor a 'bad war', but an empty war. I did nothing of significance in it, and was not asked to. Those were the least satisfactory years in my life.

And boredom can be reinforced and compounded by depressingly persistent discomfort. George Orwell participated in the militia forces during the 1930s Spanish Civil War, writing his vivid, unfussy account of his own experience very soon afterwards. That intimate and proximate record referred to: 'the evil atmosphere of war'; to 'the characteristic smell of war—in my experience a smell of excrement and decaying food'; to 'the lack of sleep which is inevitable even in the quietest kind of war'; and to soldiers being infested with lice:

> Down the seams of your trousers he lays his glittering white eggs, like tiny grains of rice, which hatch out and breed families of their own at horrible speed.... Glory of war, indeed! In war *all* soldiers are lousy, at least when it is warm enough. The men who fought at Verdun, at Waterloo, at Flodden, at Senlac, at Thermopylae—every one of them had lice crawling over his testicles.

'Like everyone about me'—Orwell concluded—'I was chiefly conscious of boredom, heat, cold, dirt, lice, privation, and occasional danger.'

Yet modern war has also involved exhilaration. It can be markedly exciting, as for some of those young men who fought in the Second World War, such as Lieutenant Hans-Otto Lessing: 'I am having the time of my life. I would not swap places with a king. Peacetime is going to be very boring after this!' For some, indeed, there has been a difficulty in giving up the adrenaline-fuelled high when adjusting to post-war civilian life.

And war can also offer a range of opportunities, otherwise less available or even unavailable. Basil Liddell Hart—a soldier in the First World War, and subsequently one of its most significant chroniclers—argued that modern war 'ennobles and brings out the highest in a man's character such as no other thing could' (quoted in Brian Bond's excellent edited volume, *The First World War and British Military History*). For all of its ghastliness, war's beneficent aspects should not be forgotten. Goodness, considerable bravery, kindness, morality, sexual opportunity, precious comradeship, chivalry, heroism, professional achievement and promotion, scientific innovation, and a liberation from quotidian dullness have all been variously evident and facilitated by modern war (as have opportunities, of course, for criminal enterprise, cruelty, and viciousness).

Early in Ernest Hemingway's tragic novel about the First World War, *A Farewell to Arms*, one of the characters observes that, 'There is nothing worse than war.' A handful of pages later, that same character is dead, his last moments spent screaming in terrified agony after a mortar shell has left one of his legs completely, and the other partly and hideously, severed. Like the central figure in his rough-edged novel, Hemingway himself had been a wounded ambulance-driver on the Italian front during the War; and, from Thucydides onwards, observer accounts of war have indeed been necessary and illuminating regarding the very varied lived experience of war. So it should also be noted that Hemingway's central figure, Frederic Henry, spends more time in the novel eating, drinking, and having sex than he does actually fighting. The multifarious nature of the experience of modern war should never be forgotten.

This chapter has tried very briefly to set out some of the complex and varied patterns of that world of experience. It involves different levels (the individual, the small group, the regional, the national), and an extraordinary range of engagement even across one constituency and one conflict.

Chapter 4
Legacies

> The twentieth century was the most murderous in recorded
> history. The total number of deaths caused by or associated
> with its wars has been estimated at 187 million, the equivalent
> of more than 10 per cent of the world's population in 1913.
>
> Eric Hobsbawm, Globalization, Democracy,
and Terrorism (2007)

What have modern wars achieved? War, according to Clausewitz,
'is nothing else but a mutual process of destruction', and the
central achievement of modern war has tragically been to destroy.
The devastation of the First World War has already been alluded
to, its human cost alone involving in the region of 8.5 million dead
and 21 million wounded. When set in population context, this can
perhaps appear even more cataclysmic. As Ferguson points out,
the total number of people killed in the First World War as a
percentage of 15–49-year-old available males on each side was 2.7
per cent for the Allied Powers, and an appalling 11.5 per cent for
their Central Power opponents. The Second World War saw
around 55 million people die, more of them civilian than military.
Throughout so much of modern war, mass killing, maiming, pain,
mourning, loss, emotional carnage, and psychological damage
have all been complemented by the physical destruction of
property and landscape. 'There will be no end to clearing up after
the war', as Michael Longley's 'The War Graves' phrases it.

Intra-state conflicts have had utterly shocking effect also, especially perhaps with the emergence of such frequent civil war ('armed combat within the boundaries of a recognized sovereign entity between parties subject to a common authority at the outset of the hostilities', in Kalyvas's formulation). The American Civil War of 1861–5 saw more than three million Americans fight (out of a population of a little over thirty million), while over 600,000 soldiers died in the conflict.

But, accompanying such baneful destruction has been the achievement of complex and sometimes profound political change. If war's effects are bloodily evident on the battlefield or among the victims of the violence, then they also stretch well beyond the actual bloodshed and human damage into the political and the societal. If, as argued in this book, modern war involves violence carried out with political objectives and possessing socio-political dynamics, then assessing historically the politico-social achievements of modern war will be vital. Sometimes, decisiveness can be established, as with 1815 ending the Napoleonic bid for European hegemony, or 1945 finally crushing the Nazi project. In the latter case, the war allowed for the long, subsequent control of Germany by its former adversaries; for the containment of German capacity for military aggression; for a kind of occupied national humiliation of the country at the hands of the USA, USSR, UK, and France; for the extraction of economic reparations (as well as some personal revenge and plunder by occupying forces directed against the Germans themselves); and for de-Nazification to accompany demilitarization (the war against the Nazis having, as Michael Burleigh has pointed out, 'assumed the form of a moral crusade').

War's political achievement can, however, be considerably more ambiguous too. What did conflict in the Mediterranean in the 1930s and 1940s achieve, as rivals (Italian, British, Turkish, French) attempted to rule this intriguing unit of the globe? In the end, the 'struggle for mastery' of the Mediterranean in these years concluded with a situation which was, as Simon Ball aptly puts it, 'not a great victory or a great defeat'; it was a 'blurred' rather than distinct outcome to such violence, whose main beneficiary was not the one, in any case, intended by most of the main players: 'the Italian Empire challenged the British Empire for hegemony, to the ultimate benefit of the American Empire'.

Repeated also—and resonating with our argument about the importance of the national and the state-centric in war's causation—is the fact that modern war has so often generated new national states. The post-Yugoslavian conflicts of the 1990s provide a compelling case study. The 1992–5 Bosnia-Herzegovina war, for example, did witness ghastly destruction of the kind referred to above, with 260,000 people dying, with around two-thirds of the population being displaced from their homes, with the occurrence of very extensive human rights violations (including rape, torture, and execution), and with the war-time collapse of the economy. The systematic slaughter by Bosnian Serbs of over 7,000 Bosniaks at Srebrenica in July 1995 has rightly become infamous; but vicious violence was practised in numerous directions in these wars. People displacement produced hundreds of thousands of refugees. Late on in the brutal, post-Yugoslavian cycle, the 1999 Kosovo war saw around 850,000 people leave or be forced from that territory; again, during these 1990s post-Yugoslavian wars, around 600,000 Serbs became refugees to Serbia from Croatia and Bosnia; very many others simply became missing, lost people—most of them presumably now dead, leaving thousands of terrible, plangent silences.

But, in addition to destruction, what else had been achieved here? Ethnic cleansing had produced far more homogeneous zones of residence, and seven new states had been created: Serbia, Slovenia, Croatia, Bosnia-Herzegovina, Macedonia, Montenegro, and Kosovo. The last of these (Figure 9; inhabited by around two million people) declared independence on 17 February 2008—a gesture by the majority Kosovan Albanian population, sharply rejected by Serbia, and following Kosovan attempts to establish independence in the early 1990s and a cruel, ensuing conflict. Such developments effectively produced an Albanian Kosovo—a positive result for the now-dominant majority, although one which did not necessarily resolve the region's problems. One journalist who had expertly covered the former Yugoslavia since 1991 (Tim Judah) later observed that many of the difficulties facing Kosovo at the start of the 1990s remained essentially the same nearly twenty years later, after all the blood-shedding and destruction of the conflict there. In addition to persisting enmity and division, economic difficulties have certainly remained profound. And yet the Kosovan pursuit of self-determination had indeed seen the region purged not only of Serbian power, but also of many actual Serbs themselves, and of the Serbian imprint on visual, institutional, and physical culture in Kosovo. In essence, most of Kosovo became Albanian; and this represented a desirable change wrought through violence, as far as many in the population were concerned.

So the post-Yugoslav wars did end up with independence for various former Yugoslavian regional groupings, a brutally achieved pattern of neater match between population and dominant regime emerging after the wars; as Wolfe puts it, 'the fact that seven states emerged where there once had been only one conveyed the indisputable message that violence to further the cause of nationhood . . . can be effective'. Despite the horror, some stability and some limited justice had accompanied this ethno-national carvery. So Serbia's non-Kosovo population in 2002 was in the region of 7.5 million, of whom the overwhelming majority was indeed Serbian; yet Slobodan Milošević, Serbia's war-time leader, had fallen from power on 5 October 2000 and died while in custody in The Hague during his trial on 11 March 2003.

Even if not creating new states or nations, war can intensify existing national loyalties, identities, and commitments. There

9. The post–Yugoslavian states

might be nothing automatic or inevitable about this process. But it has been historically evidenced repeatedly, with strengthened solidity of shared belonging, shared suffering, shared achievement, and shared myths of national character, uniqueness, and moral purpose. And it has often caused the further centralization of the state, for all of the latter's complexity. The first truly 'total' war (that of 1914–18) did see the effective militarization of some societies, the utilization of all possible elements of the state for the war effort, and an emblematic war-time expansion of state power and capacity. Qualifications need to be recognized also, however. True, the United Kingdom saw greater intrusiveness by the state into various aspects of its subjects' lives during the First World War; but even by the early 1920s, for example, the state had largely withdrawn from intervention in the economy again towards pre-war levels and remit.

Political changes to the contours of states have as importantly concerned their power and their relationships abroad. So what, for instance, have wars of decolonization achieved? In the case of the British Empire (the world's largest, to date), the reasons for disengagement were complex: declining economic capacity was crucial, as was the growing perception that the financial and other costs of maintaining the Empire were increasingly outweighing the benefits, in practice. Violence against Britain played a part; but so too—less obviously—did the fear of more violence elsewhere if pre-emptive concessions were not yielded. As so often in military history, the most successful violence was frequently that which did not have to be used.

Military damage to Empire could, of course, come from rivals rather than rebels. Certainly, the greatest threats to the British Empire itself were not anti-colonial rebellions, but rival imperial forces, and it was more the economic cost of fighting those rival empires than the damage inflicted by nationalist uprisings which mortally wounded British imperial hegemony. In Hobsbawm's words, 'The truth is that what brought empires to an end was rarely the revolt of their subject peoples alone'; most post-1945 transfers of power from the British Empire to local successors occurred peacefully and voluntarily, with disengagement owing as much to post-war economic weakness as to revolting colonial nationalists.

Some, such as Barnett, have developed this theme to try to explain British post-war decline on the basis partly of the experiences, choices, illusions, errors, and performance during the Second World War itself: according to such a view, a moral-romantic naivety and idealistic, economically unrealistic approach had been adopted by those running the UK during the war; there had been very poor management in industry, and a national approach which was outdated in methods, technology, leadership, and mentality; compared with its rivals, the UK therefore lacked economic competiveness. This argument has been robustly challenged, but it does demonstrate the potentially organic linkages which can exist between war-time decisions and wider societal legacies.

This involves also the acknowledgement that militaries do not so much have an impact on society but, of course, are themselves society too. So the implications of changing patterns of perceived military necessity can be huge. At the start of the 21st century the British Army contained just over 100,000 men and women; at the end of the Second World War its numbers had exceeded three million. At the start of the 21st century the UK Royal Navy contained fewer than 50,000 people in it; at the end of the Second World War, its number had exceeded 850,000. At the start of the 21st century the Royal Air Force comprised just over 50,000 personnel; at the end of the Second World War, as Thompson's *Imperial War Museum Book of Modern Warfare* also points out, it had contained over a million people. The impact of such changes on the economies of certain regions and classes within the UK, and on Britain's self-image as a people, was considerable.

Many kinds of relationship can be affected. It has often and rightly been pointed out how male an experience war-time combat has tended to be (although the exceptionality of this gender bias has sometimes, I think, been exaggerated: the percentage of classical composers in the modern period who have been women, or of professional boxers who have been female, has also been very low, for example). Argument persists about the reasons for the male orientation of the military, biological and cultural and political theses all having claims to be taken seriously, yet each offering probably only part of an ultimately fuller explanation. Yet modern war has in various key ways made dramatic changes to the gendering of opportunities and relationships. Both the First and Second World Wars witnessed occupational shifts for women (though some did not last far into peace). As the *Oxford Illustrated History of Modern War* points out, in 1914 women represented 23 per cent of the British work force in industry and transport, while in 1918 the figure had risen to 34 per cent. In 1914 women comprised 27 per cent of the British work force in trade and finance; four years later the figure was 53 per cent. Women became indispensable workers during the war, their roles were dramatically altered as a result, and in the 1918 Representation of the People Act women over thirty years of age were granted the vote. Likewise, technical and scientific innovation accompanied (and sometimes outlived in its effects) these shifts in gender opportunity, whether relating to military invention, the pioneering of psychiatry, or revolutions in communications technology.

What of war's economic effects? There are usually those who have a good war, including some within industries or businesses whose trade witnesses growth to accompany the spilled blood. But there is evidence (as in the work of Guidolin and La Ferrara) to suggest that some aspects of modern economic markets—especially in the United States—do actually thrive on the onset of violent conflict—though, of course, the impact is complex and far from uniformly, enduringly benign. Frequently, there is striking economic expansion (as with the US economy during the Second World War) and on occasions people can engage in violent conflict with the specific aim of acquiring direct material advantage, often very brutally. Yet there is economic destruction all too often also, for some sections of many war-ravaged societies, and for some economies as a whole. Eric Hobsbawm's judgement that, 'Britain was never the same again after 1918 because the country had ruined its economy by waging a war substantially beyond its resources', retains its detonating power as an assessment of modern war's baneful capacity in this regard.

Disaggregation within each state and each conflict allows for recognition also of sectional, instrumental, group, or individual advantage achieved. Sometimes war can suit the leadership of a country, party, movement, or organization. And achievements in war-time settings can involve military glory and careers as well as political ones. So the issue of war's achievement, when seen through these multi-levelled lenses, can have various layers of instrumental advantage and benefit and outcome too.

Longer legacies include the achievement or creation of some memories of war. This effect should not be taken for granted: it would be naïve to assume that even the most famous modern wars have left the clearest imprint on later generations' consciousness. Again, as Eric Hobsbawm has pointed out,

> no one who has been asked by an intelligent American student whether the phrase 'Second World War' meant that there had been a 'First World War' is unaware that knowledge of even the basic facts of the [20th] century cannot be taken for granted

and this point applies well to the wider subject of modern war too. For so much is *not* remembered about war, and what has not been changed by wars must be recalled as sharply as what has.

But the memory of war often involves an understandable but hyperbolic and misleading effort to remember necessary and decisive achievement, a brave effort to make sense of all the loss, pain, and sacrifice. In Michael Burleigh's words, 'The Great War had created a sense of mass entitlement, a feeling that all the death and suffering had to be for something'. What might this mean in detailed practice? How was the Belgian town of Ypres, for example, remembered in Britain between 1914 and 1940? Well, there was an inter-war remembrance movement called the Ypres League (founded in October 1921) which sought to sustain a permanent connection between the British Empire and the Belgian town, and to suggest that spiritual and purifying benefit might be gained by reflecting on what had been bravely sacrificed and heroically achieved at Ypres, in a perceivedly noble struggle. At Ypres in November 1914 the British Expeditionary Force had fought, and then there were the three great battles of Ypres in 1915, 1917, and 1918. Many thousands of British soldiers died there, amid horrific and appalling mass violence. But sacrifice was seen as creating spiritual benefit, and to commemorate in a certain way could be a spiritually uplifting and ennobling experience in itself. So, indeed, the British commemorating and remembering of Ypres in the post-war era presented it as (in Connelly's words) 'a place where British values of faith, loyalty, courage, and resolution were tested and never found wanting'. However partial or sentimental or reassuring some memories can be, there is an understandable attempt often to find a meaning in the awfulness of war, to understand what has happened in terms of there having been some valuable purpose to it.

Part of what war has achieved, therefore, is its indirect prompting of us to do things afterwards with a view to remembering conflict, some of these things binding people together and offering purpose and spiritual rewards in post-war attempts to make sense of appallingly brutal violence and destruction. Memory here can be invoked in an attempt to sanctify the people who sacrificed themselves in war, in a kind of soothing apotheosis. Taking inspiration from the sacrifice of the dead, there can then be a spiritual dimension bestowed upon the remembrance. Official commemorations—as well as tending to homogenize—tend in this way towards respect for the dead and for those who have sacrificed life or limb as soldiers for their country; and they lean towards presenting the best of national character in such self-sacrificing, martial commitments.

But elegiac and moving memorials can also stress worthlessness and futility. In *A Long Long Way* Sebastian Barry's fictional Willie Dunne was born in 1896: a soldier in the Royal Dublin Fusiliers, he died in the First World War at the age of twenty-one, the son of a Catholic Royal Irish Constabulary (RIC) policeman. The novel partly reflects a latter-day historiographical revolution which has seen Irish Catholic/nationalist participants in the First World War British Army remembered, after many years of politically loaded amnesia. It is a humanizing, moving depiction of the appalling suffering and then the poignant forgetting of a soldier's youthful horror and death; for many in the Great War's British Army were Irish ('It should be called the fucking Irish-British Army'), and the hideous destruction is unsentimentally imagined in Barry's depictions of the dead: 'the gashes where missing arms and legs had been, their breasts torn away, and hundreds and hundreds of floating hands, and legs, and big heavy puddles of guts and offal, all mixed through the loam and sharded vegetation'. Again, the gloriously unsentimental quality of William Orpen's wonderful First World War paintings ('Dead Germans in a Trench' (1918), for example, or 'Zonnebeke' (1918; Figure 10)), is one reason for their enduring strength of impact, even yet. Some of the greatest of artistic depictions of modern war portray unremembered remnants, long separated from love.

And, tragically, we again and again get our popular remembering of war wrong. We say 'First World War' and think of the trenches, but obviously there was so very much more to it than that, and—as Paul Fussell has suggested—that trench image simplifies and to

10. 'Zonnebeke' (1918) by Sir William Orpen

some extent distorts a fuller, more accurate memory of the war. Probably, the futility of the 1914–18 conflict—of which there was far too much—has been presented as more straightforward because of this trench near-obsession. Again, on occasions, we have been led by (and therefore towards) self-reinforcing misremembering, of a supposed heroism which evaporates on close inspection, or of an exaggerated clarity of moral justification. Sadly, the redressing of injustice is hardly the central fulcrum on which the causation of modern war has turned in most cases. As Max Hastings has rightly pointed out, even in the supposedly axiomatic instance of a just modern war, the battle against the Nazis during 1939–45, issues such as the defence of the Jews against Hitler were far less prominent among and contemporaneously motivating for the Allies than they have subsequently become in our post-war, self-comforting false memory.

And assessments of war's achievements do press us towards consideration of the moral. If (as Niall Ferguson forcibly argues) the First World War was not inevitable or if (as Paul Preston sagely hints) the Spanish Civil War is judged in the end to have been unnecessary, then moral questions are unavoidably raised for the historian and for the reader alike. The huge literature on the ethics of war—both the issue of when it might be legitimate to go to war (*jus ad bellum*), and of what it is legitimate to do in war once it has begun (*jus in bello*)—cannot be addressed fully in a chapter of this size. But the issue of morality has haunted our discussions of causation and experience and achievement alike. Some respond to the outrageous and often disproportionate horror of war by adopting pacifism, while others distinguish between (a more active) non-violence and (a more passive) pacifism, and further advocate the greater effectiveness of the former when it is compared with the supposed efficacy of violence itself. Such claims are extraordinarily difficult to assess in practice but—perhaps regrettably—they have failed to become pervasive in rooms occupied by powerful politicians.

Have such politicians been repeatedly immoral in their decision-making about going to war? Professor Sue Mendus has argued thoughtfully that politicians are not necessarily less moral than the rest of us, but that the challenges they face might make aspects of their moral choice-making more difficult. Certainly, a strong case can be made that politicians often face a tension between their own ethical commitments and the demands of an impartial morality required by their position of political responsibility, and that decisions about war fall at the sharper end of that continuum of tension.

Equally certainly, the historian looking at war will often feel humbled rather than inspired by our morally ragged species, which is not to deny the extraordinary heroism of those who have shown courage and idealism in modern war, and those who have endured loss and pain in such conflict. It is merely to acknowledge that—given the failure of justifications for war to match true causal explanation and motivation, and the failure of justification or motivation to be matched neatly by bloodily achieved outcome—we should be more hesitant than we might like, whether as states or as citizens, to engage in this most awful of human activities.

Regarding Just War thinking itself, there have been very many admirable variations on important themes, but Jean Bethke Elshtain's summary of seven key requirements on those engaging in war presents an excellent adumbration:

> (1) that a war be the last resort to be used only after all other means have been exhausted; (2) that a war be clearly an act of redress of rights actually violated or defence against unjust demands backed by the threat of force; (3) that war be openly and legally declared by properly constituted governments; (4) that there be a reasonable prospect for victory; (5) that the means be proportionate to the ends; (6) that a war be waged in such a way as to distinguish between combatants and non-combatants; (7) that the victorious nation not require the utter humiliation of the vanquished.

Moreover, the political context for making decisions about going to war, and the military setting for deciding what to do in it, both tend to be immediate and urgent rather than leisurely or scholarly. There is here what one of the sharpest thinkers on the subject, Michael Walzer, refers to as a 'practical morality'. Walzer himself suggests that war is not justified on the grounds of what states could or might do, but rather on the basis of what they are actually doing; and, more particularly, on the basis of the defence of right. But do states have a right to fight? And is the ensuing war, and the manner of fighting it in grainy practice, proportional to the cause at hand and to what can be achieved through violence? More specifically, is the cost of achieving Goal X worth the suffering of war, if something less than Goal X, but still significant, could be brought about with far less human suffering? Scholars of civil resistance (such as Roberts and Garton Ash, or Chenoweth and Stephan) have produced work which suggests, perhaps, not.

A short book such as this can only set out a case very briefly, observing synoptically that there have repeatedly been severe restrictions on what even dominant military powers and empires can achieve through war (Vietnam); that so many conflicts appear deeply futile in terms of their participants' ostensible ambitions (Iran-Iraq War 1980–8); that frequently and unsurprisingly conflicts conclude with deeply ambiguous achievement (Korea 1950–3—Stalin and Mao had wanted Kim Il-Sung to capture South Korea, and this he did not do; the UN mostly wanted the unification of Korea, and this was not achieved either; but those who wanted to resist and thwart North Korean aggression did succeed rather better); and that—despite high-sounding rhetoric—war does not necessarily result in the triumph of the virtuous or the just, all too frequently leaving instead the vilest men exalted, and the wicked walking on every side (to borrow phraseology from the *King James Bible*, Psalm 12, verse 8).

What can be done here in this short book, in some fruitful detail, is to consider two very different kinds of modern war, separated by almost a century, and to assess something of what they actually achieved (bearing in mind especially, perhaps, the points made above about proportionality).

First, then, what did the belligerent powers in the First World War achieve in practice? What did pouring out all of that Brookean red, sweet wine of youth actually bring about? Some scholars have been forthright in their answer, as with Robson on the First World War: 'None of the warring nations could honestly claim that they had accomplished the aims for which they had gone to war, because none had any avowed aims other than self-defence and victory'.

In addition to huge casualties, Germany had to disarm, pay reparations to its adversaries, see substantial territory within its borders occupied by the Allies, give up all French and Belgian land as well as all eastern European conquests acquired since 1914, and see its army greatly reduced in capacity and size (see Figure 11). Likewise, for Austria-Hungary, the War resulted in the dissolution of the Habsburg Monarchy—in addition to huge losses: even by the end of 1914 itself the Austrians had lost a million and a quarter men. For her part, Turkey lost possessions in defeat as well.

Victory did not bring unalloyed benefits to the Allies, however. France suffered such enormous losses as to constitute national devastation. The Russian regime experienced cataclysmic revolution. True, Britain acquired much new imperial territory and saw German rivalry stalled. But she had not achieved the security of empire which had been sought, and even historians richly aware of the case which can be made for the legitimacy of Britain going to war in 1914 (scholars such as Adrian Gregory), concede that the war involved staggering costs but that 'the compensations were distinctly limited'. In addition to the shocking loss of life and limb, Britain's war legacy (as we have mentioned) included economically destructive effects, with debts, inflation, and unemployment all causing huge and lasting damage.

For the War witnessed a shift in the economic balance of power from Britain and France decisively towards the United States. So, if there was an eventual winner from the 1914–18 conflict, it was a power which had been absent from the conflict at its commencement and therefore immune to charges of having started the conflagration with war aims at its outset. It is probably fair to argue that the First World War made more sense, in terms of the thwarting of German aggression, than years of understandable disillusionment have left most people tending to assume. But it is still very hard to be sure that the benefits of the conflict were significantly benign enough to have justified such a terrible holocaust.

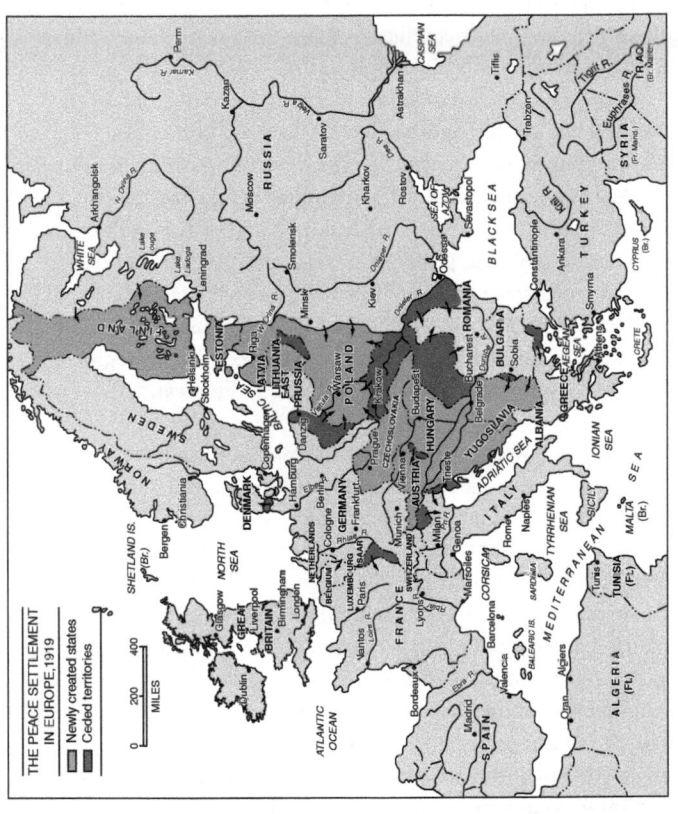

11. The peace settlement in Europe, 1919

A very different, and much lesser, conflict was embarked upon in the early-21st century by the power which had emerged to economic prominence after 1918. Following the terrorist attacks upon it of 11 September 2001 (9/11), the United States declared a War on Terror, a war which combined—as so many modern wars tellingly have done—the military with the non-military. It involved recognizably orthodox conflicts in Afghanistan and Iraq, wedded to much wider notions of struggle against a terrorist threat which had been so hideously embodied in the 9/11 atrocity. Led by the USA, the War on Terror none the less featured numerous, wide-ranging allies and although the term lost favour before the decade was out, the post-9/11 years were ones during which international relations were partly dominated by this endeavour. The War attempted to protect the US and its allies from further terrorist attacks, to capture or kill those responsible for 9/11 and to defeat al-Qaida, to extirpate all terrorist groups of international reach, and to counter the influence and power of those regimes which had supported terrorist opponents of the West.

How successful was this war and—more interestingly—why? There have been no al-Qaida strikes within the USA since 9/11, and only limited numbers of fatal attacks in Western Europe during the post-9/11 decade. That numerous terrorist schemes appear to have been planned does not mean that the threat was necessarily all that extensive, but it does demonstrate that an enduring danger had and has remained. The US authorities could legitimately point to a series of planned attacks which were foiled, including that of the shoe-bomber Richard Reid on board a flight to Miami in December 2001; of Iyman Faris (May 2003), convicted of planning to destroy Brooklyn Bridge in New York; of the plotters aiming to attack the New York Stock Exchange (August 2004); of those convicted of planning to blow up a New York subway station (August 2004); and so forth.

These successes have been complemented by some high-profile strikes against terrorist enemies, most famously the killing of

Osama bin Laden himself in May 2011; 'The world is safer. It is a better place because of the death of Osama bin Laden', as President Barack Obama decisively put it. Debate rages over how far al-Qaida has effectively been destroyed, but there is little doubt that the organization as it existed in September 2001 has been constrained and degraded and denied previously available havens and space for organization. In terms of state regimes, the Taliban were driven from power in Afghanistan, and Saddam Hussein's regime was destroyed in Iraq, although violent conflict and a measure of chaos have endured in both countries despite huge US-led efforts to prevent this in subsequent years. The threat of terrorism remains, however, and in fact the levels of global terrorist attack have risen rather than fallen during the post-9/11 period. Numerous scholars (including Berman and Stepanova) have pointed out that post-9/11 figures for terrorist incidence and fatality-generation have been depressingly high, despite the collective international efforts at counter-terrorism in recent years, and that they actually rose during the years of the War on Terror.

There can be no consensually calibrated assessment of whether the War on Terror has worked; its successes have been significant in some regards, but deeply limited in others. The important point is to think about *why* this huge undertaking has been limited and flawed to the extent that it has. I have argued elsewhere (*Terrorism: How to Respond*) that there exists an historically-grounded framework for successful wars against terrorism, comprising seven key and inter-linked elements: learn to live with it; where possible, address underlying root problems and causes; avoid the over-militarization of response; recognize that intelligence is the most vital element in successful counter-terrorism; respect orthodox legal frameworks and adhere to the democratically-established rule of law; coordinate security-related, financial, and technological preventative measures; and maintain strong credibility in counter-terrorist public argument.

The concluding section of this chapter will utilize this framework as a way of assessing why the successes and limitations of the War on Terror's achievements have been as they have. Many arguments have been offered to the effect that states typically fail to learn the lessons even of their own recent counter-terrorist experiences, when addressing contemporary crises; and some scholars have been very vocal indeed in asserting that recent counter-terrorism has proved profoundly unsuccessful in achieving its ostensible goal: 'Counter-terrorism has become self-fulfilling and it is now pivotal in *promoting* terrorism'; 'counter-terrorism has become terrorism's best ally' (Joseba Zulaika).

So, within the framework set out above, how can we evaluate and explain the efficacy or otherwise of the War on Terror?

First, learn to live with it. Most scholars would tend to agree that counter-terrorism works most effectively when it is cast in long-termist rather than short-term mode, and this is a view shared by practitioners with impressive acumen and experience in the field also ('short-termism is a big, big risk'—Judith Gillespie, Police Service of Northern Ireland Deputy Chief Constable, interviewed by the author, Belfast, 15 April 2011). There is no doubting the committed engagement of the US and its allies to fighting a long war, post-9/11. Yet some of what was done does now seem to have been hubristically ambitious. Scholarly recognition that, in Robert Goodin's wording, 'Terrorists will be with us for the foreseeable future' casts a sceptical shadow across statements from President George W. Bush in September 2001 that 'we will rid the world of evildoers' (quoted in Brahimi's excellent study, *Jihad and Just War*) and that 'our war begins with al-Qaida but it does not end there'; rather, it would 'not end until every terrorist group of global reach has been found, stopped and defeated' (as quoted by Jason Burke).

Sir David Omand (UK Intelligence and Security Coordinator under Prime Minister Tony Blair during 2002–5) has sagely recognized that the goal, regarding terrorism, should be that of 'reducing the risk' rather than 'eliminating it' (quoted by Steve Hewitt), and the dangers of promising a victory which cannot be delivered are plain and self-damaging enough. War aims should be achievable.

This involves being realistic about what can be done, and therefore also about what cannot: though it is politically difficult to keep saying it, terrorist attacks will remain a possibility and—on occasions—a reality. But they must be kept within reasonable proportion. States have tended often to endure resiliently in the face of violence which, in sum, is reasonably unthreatening; and terrorist campaigns tend to become less able to shock or compel, the longer that they persist.

So the question arises about proportionality of response to this ongoing yet comparatively manageable threat. The War on Terror was hugely expensive. Figures are hard to establish precisely, but estimates include claims such as those by Jackson *et al* that the War had cost the USA $864 billion by 2008, and by Mueller and Stewart that US spending on domestic security in the decade after 9/11 rose by over $1 trillion. Given the scale of terrorist threat globally (with the 21st-century annual number of terrorist incidents *worldwide* comfortably falling under 2,000 per annum, many of them comparatively minor), it seems hard to avoid the charge of disproportionate reaction during the War on Terror.

Second, where possible, address underlying root problems and causes. In the wake of terrorist atrocity or in the midst of seeming terrorist crisis, it is understandable for states and citizens under attack not to want to focus on the root causes behind the violence, since this can seem to lend legitimacy to those who have generated such carnage. But—emotionally painful though it is to acknowledge this at times—terrorist violence tends to emerge from the roots of serious political problems, and winning a war against it will not be made more likely by ignoring or misdiagnosing its causes. In the wake of 9/11, the War on Terror witnessed much rhetoric devoted to rather casual religious explanations for jihadism, and to shallow clash-of-civilizations arguments, and less attention was given than might have been fruitful to the real dynamics behind what turned out to be largely unpopular terrorism, as far as most Muslims globally were concerned. Accurately explaining why terrorism has emerged does not imply giving its perpetrators what they demand. In fact, a more common pattern has probably been that terrorist campaigns have ended on the basis of political arrangements far *short* of what terrorist activists have sought, but sufficient for most of their supposed constituency to accept (hardly a vindication of terrorism, in truth).

The USA's key ally in the War on Terror, the United Kingdom, developed an integrated strategy regarding prevention and response, and one whose evolution is illuminating here. Work started on the CONTEST (COuNter-TErrorism STrategy) in 2002, it was adopted in 2003, published in 2006, and an updated CONTEST2 was then published in 2009. It involved four complementary, alliteratively designated elements: *Pursue* (stopping terrorist attacks, disrupting terrorist networks, investigating and detecting attacks); *Prevent* (stopping people becoming terrorists or supporting terrorism in the first place); *Protect* (strengthening the UK's protection against terrorist attack and reducing national vulnerability); and *Prepare* (being prepared to lessen the impact of terrorist attacks in those cases in which an incident has not been prevented, and strengthening post-attack recovery).

One of the most intriguing aspects of this explicitly counter-terrorist strategy was its attention to causes and motivations; the June 2011 iteration of *Prevent* had the government declare that 'the main aim of *Prevent* must be to prevent people from becoming terrorists or supporting terrorism' in the first place. But this revised version stepped back from previous government policy somewhat, in separating more clearly the promotion of societal integration from counter-terrorism as such: 'the government will not securitize its integration strategy. This has been a mistake in the past.'

For addressing root causes means identifying what those causes actually are, and what can be done about them. In the UK case, it was arguably not a lack of societal integration which lay at the root of the 21st-century terrorist threat. The fact that over 30 per cent of those convicted for al-Qaida-associated terrorist offences in the United Kingdom during 1999–2009 attended university or a higher education institution, with a further 15 per cent having studied or attained a vocational or further education qualification (*Prevent* 2011), if anything suggests a rather high degree of integration, in fact.

A much more plausible source of rage leading to actual terrorist violence centred on UK and Western foreign policy, and especially the military endeavours in the wars in Afghanistan and Iraq. Our third principle for effective counter-terrorism is to avoid the over-militarization of response. After 9/11 there was an understandable rage on the part of the USA, a desire to demonstrate that the state would commit itself muscularly to protecting its people and their interests, and a reasonable enough conviction that something had to be done about the Afghanistan base from which al-Qaida had prepared for the attacks (Figure 12).

So when President George W. Bush responded to 9/11 with an emphatically military response, it was not without some basis in understandable instinct and reasoned reaction. For one thing, Bush's now often-maligned strategy against terrorism actually strengthened his popularity in regard to re-election as president of the United States. But even in terms of countering terrorism itself there could be seen to be some positive effects of the militarized engagement. The Taliban regime, which controlled most of Afghanistan in 2001 and whose leader (Mullah Omar) decided to

12. Coalition forces in Afghanistan: 'Operation Enduring Freedom'

protect Osama bin Laden rather than hand him over to the USA, had indeed provided al-Qaida with a vital base of operations. The US-led 'Operation Enduring Freedom' (which had more than sixty countries supporting it in international coalition), speedily overthrew Taliban control, with attacks beginning on 7 October, Kabul falling on 13 November, and Kandahar following on 7 December. The war model had yielded results, and promptly, with al-Qaida's safe haven in Afghanistan being substantially closed off.

The thinking behind this war had been clear enough. As the then UK Prime Minister Tony Blair later put it, 'The analysis we had was that Afghanistan had been a failed state; the Taliban had taken over; and as a consequence extremism under their protection was allowed to grow'. Something had had to be done, and emphatically *had* been done, with real damage being inflicted on al-Qaida. There had been Allied counter-terrorist successes in post-9/11 Afghanistan which had saved lives in the UK. And on 23 November 2011 (ten years on from the start of the Afghan venture) the head of the UK armed forces, General Sir David Richards, suggested that 'we will all agree in ten years' time that this was a necessary war and we've come out of it with our heads held high. The British armed forces [will be] held in huge respect around the world for doing the right thing and fighting hard for those freedoms, and it will be seen to have been worth it not just by us but by everybody.' Clearly, this had not been without terrible costs: during that decade 389 UK soldiers had been killed in the Afghan war, and a further 540 seriously injured. But it would be hard to deny that there had been a need to do something to protect against Taliban-based al-Qaida atrocity, or to deny that some serious progress had indeed been made.

The difficulty with the Afghan war was that so much else—so much which was negative—also accompanied these hard-earned gains. Taliban power was removed, but the Taliban regrouped and a lengthy and very bloody conflict then ensued. Within this, predictably, military means gave gifts to jihadist terrorists in the form of collateral damage against Muslim civilians. As reported in *USA Today*, on 28 August 2008, US officials admitted that in 2007 alone US air strikes had killed 321 Afghan civilians, while the initially insensitive approach by the soldiers and their isolation from local people—together with the violence—unquestionably proved counter-productive. Anti-Western insurgents gained strength and momentum, the number of insurgent-initiated attacks increasing around 400 per cent between 2002 and 2006 according to Jones; according to the US military itself, there were around thirty security incidents per week in Afghanistan in 2004, and 300 a week by the summer of 2008. By October 2008 the UK's then most senior military commander in Afghanistan, Brigadier Mark Carleton-Smith, acknowledged that a decisive military victory over the Taliban was not going to happen. Managing the insurgency, rather than defeating it, was the more sensible goal, he suggested.

Complex motivation lay behind these hybrid insurgents, including a desire for revenge for violence by the occupying forces and a zeal to expel them from the country, to overthrow the new Kabul government, and to establish a religiously different (and more stringently Islamic) social order. The theme of Muslim violence to avenge anti-Muslim, Western aggression was strong. As one Taliban military commander put it in February 2006, 'We are not fighting here for Afghanistan, but we are fighting for all Muslims everywhere and also the Mujahideen in Iraq. The infidels attacked Muslim lands and it is a must that every Muslim should support his Muslim brothers' (Mullah Dadullah, quoted by Jones). Implicit here is one of the key difficulties with the wars of the War on Terror: US and UK foreign policy, justified and prompted partly by a desire to undermine jihadist terrorism, could also serve to intensify much of the anger which generated that very terrorism, and indeed could seem to some to vindicate the anti-Western, violent arguments proffered by jihadists.

Despite his continuing conviction that the Afghan policy had been the right one, even Tony Blair came to be clear too about there having been some misjudgement behind this venture:

> I certainly misjudged the depth of the failure of the Afghanistan state; and the ability of the Taliban to immerse themselves into the local communities, particularly in the south, and to call upon reinforcements from across the border in the mountainous highlands that seemed a law unto themselves. Thus immersed, they were able by a continuation of intimidation, organization, and sheer malevolence to reassert control of parts of the territory, or at least to disrupt the work we were doing.

By 2009, much of the priority of Western forces in Afghanistan was the circular one of simple force protection, each day trying centrally to protect themselves. One of the factors which compounded Allied difficulty was the variously distracting and awkward engagement, from 2003, in Iraq, in the other main military arena for the War on Terror. The deceptive ease with which initial military victory had appeared to be achieved in the war in Afghanistan probably enhanced the hubristic mood in Washington, and the prior zeal to do something about Iraq was thus reinforced, especially in a setting in which post-9/11 counter-terrorism could be used as the flag of justification.

In terms of countering terrorism, however, Iraq was of far less significant benefit than Afghanistan, and in this sense it is unfortunate that the two conflicts are so often conflated in public debate. Iraq certainly did make effective work in Afghanistan more difficult, for several reasons. Operation Iraqi Freedom distracted and drew away from Afghanistan both cash and also people who were crucial to a properly expert application of strategy there, including personnel with linguistic and local experience (something confirmed by Michael Scheuer, head of the CIA's bin Laden unit during 1996–9). In November 2011 General David Richards, head of the UK's armed forces, frankly admitted that 'Iraq did take our eye off the Afghanistan ball'.

But the Iraq War was presented by Washington as a front line in the War on Terror (Figure 13). Did this militarized approach work well? Like Afghanistan, Iraq had been a site of long-tangled roots of competing divisions and conflicts, and the preparation for post-war politics by the US and its allies was rather naïve and inadequate. The initial phase of military success was indeed striking, with the war to remove the Saddam Hussein regime being quickly won: 20 March 2003 saw the attack begin; on 9 April Baghdad was secured by the coalition forces. But ensuing collateral damage to Iraqi civilians then exacerbated the difficulties faced, as did the collapse of order and economy in parts of the country after the invasion. Hussein himself was indeed duly captured (14 December 2003) and executed, but since the pretexts for the war had been to dismantle weapons of mass destruction (WMD) which were never found, and to react to Hussein's supposed (but non-existent) role in al-Qaida's atrocity against the USA, the war aims were rather evaporative. It could be said that US control was enhanced in a region of high

13. Twenty-first century war in Iraq

economic and military significance; but even here the costs were high, and instability rendered the achievement less than clear.

The United States lost credibility after the WMD embarrassment, and acquired a certain amount of international opprobrium and isolation. Moreover, the long and painful conflict which followed the initial US-led victory in 2003 proved very bruising. Wesley Gray, a US Marine Corps adviser working with the Iraqi army in 2006–7, made clear the difficulties faced by even the world's dominant superpower in combating determined insurgents, reflecting the limitations on what can be achieved in war, even by such great powers: 'Roughly 20 per cent of every American's tax bill goes to the defence budget. And yet a bunch of relatively uneducated sheepherders with twenty bucks can kick our asses all over Iraq'. The horrors of Saddam Hussein's appalling regime should not be forgotten; but neither should the blood spilled in the years from March 2003 onwards. As reflected by Jackson *et al*, by the summer of 2010 some estimates suggested a post-invasion civilian death toll alone in Iraq of around 100,000 people; by the same year over 6,000 coalition troops and private contractors had been killed.

Moreover, as part of the explicit War on *Terror*, it is hard to see the Iraq venture as having achieved enough to justify its costs at all. Scholarly opinion seems repeatedly to affirm such a view. Wilkinson:

> Whatever the rights and wrongs of the invasion of Iraq it could hardly be claimed as a major victory against al-Qaida—on the contrary; it provided a gratuitous propaganda gift to bin Laden, who could portray the invasion as an act of Western imperialism against the Muslim world. More recruits could be mobilized for al-Qaida's 'holy war', and more donations could be obtained from al-Qaida's wealthy backers.

Crenshaw: 'The occupation of Iraq inspired further terrorism from al-Qaida and its allies and affiliates'; Richardson: the Iraq War 'has radicalized a whole generation of young jihadists who have been led to believe that the US is establishing a base in the Middle East with which to exploit the resources and dominate the politics of the region'. Moreover, this development (that invading Iraq would stimulate and—for some—further justify jihadism), was a likelihood sharply anticipated in advance by US and UK intelligence services, and recognized clearly by them after the event.

Counter-terrorist practitioners tend to resonate here with academic observers. Michael Scheuer, who had been head of the CIA's Osama bin Laden unit between 1996 and 1999, has argued that post-9/11 US foreign policy 'generates Islamist insurgents faster than they can be killed'; Sir David Omand, the UK's very able Intelligence and Security Coordinator at the time of the invasion, has been equally frank: 'The intervention in Iraq was further stoking up passions and attracting further supporters for the al-Qaida world view'; the Director-General of the UK Security Service (MI5) during 2002–7, Eliza Manningham-Buller, was clear that the Iraq War had helped to radicalize many British Muslims and that it had worsened the threat of terrorist attack in the UK itself—she told the UK Iraq War Inquiry on 20 July 2010 that the security services had become 'overwhelmed' by the increased threat posed by home-grown terrorists, who thought that the West had an anti-Muslim policy; asked how much the UK's involvement in the Iraq War had led to an increased terrorist threat in the United Kingdom, Manningham-Buller replied: 'substantially'.

For, after the Iraq War had commenced, it was indeed easier for al-Qaida and their allies to claim that their own jihadist violence was legitimately defensive and reactive to Western brutality against and wrongs against Muslims. So levels of fatal jihadist terrorist violence by Islamic groups rose dramatically after the invasion; the threat to the West was deepened and, of course, terrorist-style violence within Iraq itself grew extraordinarily: as Peter Bergen has pointed out, 'more suicide attacks were conducted in Iraq between 2003 and 2007 than had taken place in every other country of the world combined since 1981'.

The point of this discussion has not been to present the Afghan and Iraq Wars as identical in justification or nature, nor to suggest that they were without serious rationale or substantial achievement. Rather, the point is to establish that, in terms of their declared part as wars within a War on Terror, their counter-productive dynamics partly help to explain why that latter war was marred by so many frustrations. For the Afghanistan and Iraq wars of the early 21st century do fit a pattern well established by the scholarly literature on counter-terrorism, regarding the fact that military methods are not especially effective in dealing with terrorism itself, certainly not when deployed as the main means of response. In this sense, the heavily militarized emphasis of the post-9/11 US-led War on Terror was almost certainly ill-judged. Too many gifts were simply given to terrorists, not least in terms of generating hostile public opinion; there is much evidence for this in relation to attitudes towards the USA in a range of Muslim countries in the wake of large-scale US engagement in Iraq and Afghanistan.

Even some who had famously decided to use military muscle in the fight against terrorism have at times acknowledged its unanticipated costs. Regarding his post-9/11 policies, Tony Blair referred to his choice to confront terrorism 'militarily. I still believe that was the right choice, but the costs, implications, and consequences were far greater than any of us, and certainly me, could have grasped on that day'. And it is arguable that a police-based response might, broadly, be much more appropriate to our actual terrorist threat. Terrorism should, I suspect, generally lie within the realm of professional police and intelligence agencies, a point backed up by Michael Sheehan (former New York City Deputy Commissioner for Counter-Terrorism, quoted by Mueller and Stewart): 'The most important work in protecting our country since 9/11 has been accomplished with the capacity that was in place when the event happened, not with any of the new capability bought since 9/11.'

This leads us to our fourth point regarding the War on Terror, as read through the lenses of our seven-point framework: recognize that intelligence is the most vital element in successful counter-terrorism. Again, practitioner and academic arguments tend to coincide here, and the importance of gathering and (with acumen) interpreting high-grade intelligence provides a necessary basis for knowing who one's terrorist opponents are, what they actually want, where their strengths and weaknesses and divisions lie, what they are planning to do and when and where, why they are doing what they do, and why they might stop. As David Omand has sagely put it,

> Good pre-emptive intelligence can reassure the community by removing the extremists and by disrupting potential attacks without having to fall back on the sort of blunt discriminatory measures that alienate moderate support within the community on which effective policing and counter-terrorism depends.

Yet, staggeringly, US intelligence operations were deeply and damagingly flawed in Iraq (both initially after the 2003 invasion, and also beforehand), and in Afghanistan (again, in the immediate wake of 2001, and also before the invasion), and also beyond these wars in the broader post-9/11 War on Terror. After the Soviet Union had left Afghanistan, there occurred little US intelligence gathering there for a decade; had there been more such work, it is possible that 9/11 would not have occurred.

Fifth, effective counter-terrorist policies should respect orthodox legal frameworks and adhere to the democratically-established rule of law. In the aftermath of such an egregious atrocity as 9/11, there is an entirely understandable urge to dispense with the normal restraints which govern democratic states and their deployment of legal protections and protocols. Yet history suggests that adherence to one's restraining rules and legal frameworks probably serves one better in countering non-state terrorism. For one thing, many terrorists have emerged, radicalized and enraged, from states which deny political and civil and human rights liberties. In her careful evaluation of counter-terrorism, Laura Donohue has concluded that the best policy for states in responding legally to terrorist challenges is to adopt 'a culture of restraint', to pass measures under extraordinary procedures 'only in the rarest of circumstances', to ensure proper mechanisms of accountability, and to resist the expansion of executive power into the judicial realm. Overall, there is much evidence to suggest that transgression against democratically established legal rules and practices is both morally dubious and also practically counter-productive.

Much that has occurred in the US-led War on Terror has indeed reflected an attachment to proper legal process. Criticisms could be levelled at the USA PATRIOT Act introduced at the end of October 2001 (the Uniting and Strengthening America by Providing Appropriate Tools Required to Intercept and Obstruct Terrorism Act), which did indeed extend state power considerably. Increased surveillance was now facilitated, in the realm of intercepting emails, investigating people's bank accounts, monitoring their telephone calls, and allowing for the deportation of immigrants accused of raising money for terrorist groups. But the scale of the 9/11 atrocity was such that it seems to me that establishing a legal framework for greater surveillance was not, in itself, necessarily misjudged; and it should be recognized that the extension of such powers does on occasions save lives in the battle against terrorist violence.

But some of the developments in the War on Terror clearly moved well beyond this, and probably with results more negative than positive in the longer term. As Bergen and others have shown, coercive interrogation methods blurred into torture on occasion, and the transgression of key human rights and proper legal practices was also evident in cases of arbitrary detention, extra-judicial killing, the maintenance of secret prisons, and the repeated mistreatment of detainees.

The problem lies not merely with the contemporary damage done to the battle against terrorism, though that can be serious enough in a contest in which public opinion is a vital resource. Allegations of torture, or of complicity in torture, can damage the credibility of the liberal democratic state as it opposes illiberal terrorist adversaries. This was the case with claims publicly made regarding al-Qaida suspects arrested during 2003–7 and allegedly tortured by Pakistan's Inter-Services Intelligence (ISI), before then being questioned by a UK Security Service allegedly aware of and therefore supposedly complicit in this prior torture (*Guardian*, 4 February 2009). While the UK authorities emphatically deny that they have in fact condoned torture, allegations of collusion in the practice have been persistent and damaging, as have similar allegations made against the CIA (*Daily Telegraph*, 4 April 2009; *Observer*, 22 February 2009; *New York Times*, 24 March 2009).

But the most lasting damage will probably only become clear in later generations. I suspect that, in fifty years' time, most of the acts of appalling aggression by non-state terrorists against Western states during the first years of the 21st century will have been forgotten, and will not be greatly discussed, but that the much less nasty events at Guantánamo Bay and Abu Ghraib Prison during the War on Terror will be remembered, repeatedly discussed, re-broadcast in detail, and used as a way of undermining the record of the liberal democratic state which oversaw them.

Guantánamo Bay detention centre was established as an effective internment camp (at a US military facility in Cuba) shortly after 9/11, to house people who were suspected of involvement with al-Qaida. Near the USA, but beyond the reach of orthodox US laws such as the right to appeal one's imprisonment, Guantánamo allowed for detention and interrogation with suspects being held indefinitely without trial and without Geneva Conventions protection. Some of those held at the centre were innocent (though it should be stressed that some were certainly not). But, in any case, the very public and publicized process of a Western power holding Muslim detainees in humiliating circumstances, without the rules of legal protection on which the USA so rightly prided itself, was extremely harmful to the US cause in its War against Terror, especially given the strong evidence emerging of repeated beatings of those being detained (*Observer*, 22 February 2009). A BBC opinion poll in 2007 found that, of over 26,000 people across twenty-five countries, seven out of ten disapproved of the way in which detainees at Guantánamo were being treated (quoted in Peter Bergen's very valuable *Longest War*).

The view that Guantánamo has been counter-productive has been agreed now by a wide range of leading authorities. When the Abu Ghraib story emerged in 2004, a similar pattern seemed likely. Formerly a jail used brutally and murderously by Saddam Hussein's regime, Abu Ghraib Prison on the western outskirts of Baghdad was reopened in August 2003 by the USA as a holding centre both for people from the former Iraqi regime and also for common criminals. By the end of 2003, it held around 7,000 inmates. The US administration initially denied any mistreatment of people held there, but in April 2004 pictures of the abuse of prisoners by US military personnel became public. Methods included hooding, sleep deprivation, the use of stress positions, intimidation using dogs, sexual humiliation, kicking and punching and beating, stripping prisoners naked, using low-voltage electric shocks, and chaining people to walls.

The reality is that sections of the Iraq prison regime under the United States dispensation had degenerated into a chaotic situation, with little oversight of what was happening and inadequate guidelines for what should and should not be done. The events at Abu Ghraib were sadistic and nasty and gained little for the authorities, while they did do lasting damage to America's reputation in the War on Terror and beyond, and will probably continue to do so long after most people have become unable to name even a single victim of post-9/11 al-Qaida terrorism. For Abu Ghraib seemed very publicly to show a profound US disrespect for Muslims and Arabs. And, given that humiliation at the hands of the West was one of the key reasons for anti-Western terrorism in the first place, and that the Iraq War had been presented as a means of limiting such terrorism, this episode represented an egregious blunder.

The sixth key principle to which we should adhere if we are to succeed in fighting a war on non-state terrorism is to coordinate security-related, financial, and technological preventative measures. Necessarily, counter-terrorism will involve difficult coordination issues within as well as between states, and there has been much improvement since 9/11 in this regard. The PATRIOT Act facilitated a better transfer of information in the USA between the FBI and the CIA; after the 7 July 2005 attacks in London, there emerged a more fully coordinated approach within the UK too; despite some well-publicized problems, US–European intelligence co-operation has made some progress in the post-9/11 years. Again, in the post-9/11 decade the European Union as such became much more energetic in the counter-terrorist field, and some significant intra-Union cooperation and coordination have occurred. But, as Javier Argomaniz has carefully shown, terrorism has continued to be seen very often through national rather than cross-national lenses within the EU, and many problems of consistency have remained across the Union; predictably, different states' goals have at times conflicted with one another, and trust has not always been ascendant. There persists a tension between the national and the EU supranational levels of action regarding terrorism, and this tension is likely to continue into the short- and medium-term future.

Of course, problems of coordination in the War on Terror are no more likely to be finally resolved than are coordination issues in other complex areas of human endeavour, and it is important to be realistic about what can be done. None the less, the EU example does remind us that some key problems have persisted. Inter-state cooperation was deeply damaged after 9/11 by some of the actions taken by the US and its allies. Moreover, although great progress has been made in some coordinating efforts within the US itself, there remain major questions about how well-conceived some of this has been. At the very least, the coordination of the vast increase in spending on Homeland Security since 9/11 seems only questionably to have produced sufficiently effective results—Mueller and Stewart: 'by any reasonable cost-benefit standard, a great deal of money seems to have been misspent and would have been far more productive—saved far more lives—if it had been expended in other ways'; 'Most enhanced homeland security expenditures since 9/11 fail a cost-benefit assessment, it seems, some spectacularly so, and it certainly appears that many billions of dollars have been misspent'. Here, as so often in counter-terrorism, the judgement is that the avoidance of over-reaction would be the most sage approach to adopt: 'avoiding over-reaction, which requires no expenditure whatever, is by far the most cost-effective counter-terrorism measure imaginable'.

Finally, how has the War on Terror fared in relation to the challenge to maintain strong credibility in counter-terrorist public argument? Both among the constituency from which your terrorist opponents putatively draw support, and among one's own more natural constituents, credibility and associated legitimacy represent truly vital resources. In the face of terrorist threats there is often a pressure to exaggerate and to misrepresent, to offer specious justifications for responses, and to lose credibility as a consequence; there has certainly been evidence of this in the record of the War on Terror. Asking why the perpetrators attacked the United States on 9/11, then

President George W. Bush answered in this fashion: 'Why do they hate us? . . . They hate our freedoms—our freedom of religion, our freedom of speech, our freedom to vote and assemble and disagree with one another' (as quoted in Bergen). In reality, a more serious mixture of hostility towards US and other Western policy in the Muslim world, particular anger against perceivedly apostate Islamic regimes, a desire to avenge prior humiliation at the hands of the West, a desire for an Islamic renaissance, and fulfilment of a set of individualized rewards more credibly explained the atrocity.

As set out in 2001 and beyond, the War on Terror itself lacked credibility in other ways too. Defeating every terrorist organization possessing global reach was almost certainly an unattainable objective, with even President Bush himself seeming eventually to acknowledge that the War on Terror could not be won.

Even the phrase itself came to be seen as unhelpful. During 2006 UK officials quietly stopped using it, and in January 2009 UK Foreign Secretary David Miliband went as far as to suggest that the term 'War on Terror' had given a misleading 'impression of a unified, transnational enemy, embodied in the figure of Osama bin Laden and al-Qaida', whereas the terrorist reality was disparate: 'The more we lump terrorist groups together and draw the battle lines as a simple binary struggle between moderates and extremists, or good and evil, the more we play into the hands of those seeking to unify groups with little in common.' The phrase 'War on Terror' also unhelpfully 'implied that the correct response was primarily military', Miliband argued. This article was published just before the Bush administration was replaced by Barack Obama's in Washington, DC, the subsequent Obama regime itself downplaying War on Terror rhetoric in practice, and effectively dropping the phrase.

Perhaps the most damaging aspect of the War on Terror in relation to Western credibility involved the war in Iraq. More specifically, the manner of justifying this supposedly integral front in the War on Terror did lasting damage to US credibility. For none of the three main foundations for justifying the war seemed genuinely persuasive.

First, it was claimed that Hussein posed a grave threat because of his Weapons of Mass Destruction, but the US intelligence community had in fact overestimated Iraq's WMD programme in 2002, and the UK's intelligence reporting was also seriously flawed. Saddam in fact posed less of a threat to the wider world than pre-war rhetoric from Bush and Blair had suggested; the information and sources upon which US estimates about Iraqi WMD had been based were, in reality, lamentably unreliable—as the Secretary of State at the time of the invasion, Colin Powell, angrily acknowledged after the fact. But Colin Powell himself had claimed in advance of the war that Iraq definitely possessed chemical and biological WMD and that Saddam was prepared to use them. This turned out to be false, very embarrassingly so when the much-anticipated WMD were not found in Iraq after the war. (A stronger argument seemed to me to be that Hussein was deeply hostile to the West, that he *wanted* to develop his WMD capacity, and that it would be wiser to destroy his regime before he possessed such weapons capacity; but that approach would have had much less effect on the public in terms of persuading them of the necessity of a pre-emptive, defensive, Hobbesian attack on Iraq.)

The second, related justification for the Iraqi adventure was that Hussein was linked to and in league with al-Qaida and other terrorist groups and that his supposed WMD threat was therefore even more alarming. As US Deputy Secretary Paul Wolfowitz put it in May 2002, 'we can't wait until there's a 9/11 with a nuclear weapon or a biological or chemical weapon to then go and find the perpetrator' (quoted in Stuart Croft's reflective book, *Culture, Crisis, and America's War on Terror*). The Bush administration presented Saddam's regime as being directly connected to and allied with al-Qaida, and managed to persuade large numbers (for a time, the majority) of Americans that his Iraqi regime had supported al-Qaida and had, indeed, been directly involved in the 9/11 attacks, something which was not in fact true. George W. Bush (2004): 'The reason I keep insisting that there was a relationship between Iraq and Saddam and al-Qaida, is because there was a relationship between Iraq and al-Qaida' (again, as quoted in Croft).

Eventually, the Bush administration conceded that there was indeed no evidence linking Hussein and Iraq to 9/11, and that Saddam and al-Qaida had not in fact been in league with one another. Indeed, Osama bin Laden had actually long been hostile—and had long been *known* to be hostile—to Saddam Hussein.

The third argument, that Saddam's was a brutal regime and that, as a tyrant, he had to be deposed and his people liberated from his grasp, stumbled up against the fact that the US did not depose all brutal tyrants and that it had, indeed, been on good terms with Hussein himself when it had seemed politic to be so.

None of this is to say that there were no benefits from the Iraq War, nor that there were no strong arguments for it. It *is* to say that the terms in which the case for the Iraq war were made, as an integral and necessary part of the War on Terror, lacked credibility in such a way as to damage—lastingly—the US and its allies' arguments in subsequent years. Credibility was lost as a consequence, and it will probably prove hard to reclaim.

This chapter has here attempted not to calibrate the success of the War on Terror in metrics-based, mechanical terms but rather to assess—against an historically informed framework regarding counter-terrorism—why some of its failings emerged as they did. There have been huge successes in the post-9/11 battle against terrorism. But in transgressing the above seven principles for effective counter-terrorism, the US and its anti-terror warrior allies did much to undermine the effectiveness of their important war. And this reinforces the broader point hinted at in this chapter: that the complex political, economic, social, and other changes achieved in war are not only bought at a destructively appalling price, but have all too often in recent history been purchased in clumsily (and avoidably) counter-productive manner.

Conclusion: war, terrorism, and future research

Concluding the writing of a book on modern war can leave one feeling something of the helpless, quasi-nihilistic poignancy so brilliantly evoked in Graham Greene's depiction of post-Second World War Vienna in *The Third Man*. The eyes feel 'flat and tired'; the mood is one of 'sad patience'; there is disenchantment with things and people previously holding us in thrall; in the end it seems 'an ugly story', 'grim and sad'; 'Poor all of us, when you come to think of it'.

But, despite the depressing historical reality of modern war and the near-certainty of its continuation in terrible fashion into the future, a more positive attitude to strike is that of asking how best we might frame future research into this vital subject. In this brief Conclusion, I want to set out what seem to me three important difficulties with researching the topic at present, and to hint at practical ways of addressing them in our future research agenda.

The first problem is the unhelpful fragmentation of the research field on modern war. It is hugely beneficial to us that so much research has been pioneered on the topic, with such increasingly professional expertise and acumen. But it is now so divided a field as to make synoptic readings and understandings of the phenomenon incredibly difficult. There is fragmentation between case study specialists and wide-angled generalizers; between students of different periods, or of different regions of the world;

between divergent academic disciplines; within academic disciplines, between competing sub-disciplinary fields of specialism (within international relations, for instance, between the empirically oriented and the theoretically inclined); and between those seeking purely an academic audience and those aiming at public scholarship.

The problem is reflected in this current book, whether through the range of disciplines on which it has had simultaneously to draw (history, political science, international relations, sociology, philosophy, anthropology, economics, theology, psychology, literary studies, law), or through the fact that so many areas of the world have effectively lain silent in its pages. Clearly, a short book has to have omissions; equally obviously, there might be judged some merit in even a short book such as this at least attempting to step out of one academic trench and to draw widely on different scholarly traditions as I have done.

But more must be done about this fragmentation, to try to bring together for us all what has become an unhelpfully fractured, divided area of study. For the fragmentation is compounded because, as argued here in this book, modern war cannot be understood except as something which is integrated into other major phenomena—nationalism, the state, empire, religion, economics, terrorism—with each of these related subjects then possessing its own specialist literature, all of which are themselves vast and professionally consuming.

So what is to be done? I think humility on the part of the various academic disciplines involved, and a consequent methodological pluralism of approach by us all, is probably a necessary starting place. Historians must acknowledge (on the basis of extensive reading) the conceptual sharpness, the hypothesis-driven argumentative power, the systematically comparative analysis, and the statistically precise methodological ambition characteristic of so many high-grade political scientists. The latter must celebrate (again, on the basis of deep immersion in the relevant literature) historians' important emphasis on the contingent, the contextually complex, the individually determined, and the unique. Historians and political scientists alike must recognize that explanations of religion will be attenuated unless they take into account the deep learning and specific acumen of theologians. Philosophers and historians should engage in more sustained, organic dialogue (and more methodological sharing) with one another than currently occurs, when they address common research problems regarding warfare. And so on around the customarily rather fissiparous academy.

This will have implications for how much scholars and others read, for the nature of the bibliographies which they develop and in which they immerse themselves, for the methodological manner in which they train the next generation of scholars, and for the organization of university centres and departments (and their seminar and lecture series, and conferences, and journals). Polarization will continue, and unhelpfully so, unless such deliberate efforts are made. Currently, many bibliographies in the field remain depressingly innocent of the kind of insights established on other parts of the university campus than their authors' own.

And progress can simultaneously be made at an individual level also. The repeated fragmentation between micro-level specialists and macro-level argumentation about violence can be challenged, if scholars are prepared bravely to test wide-angled arguments about war against truly detailed, first-hand knowledge of particular historical conflicts. This remains more rare than it should be, but the work of Wilson and Weinstein (referred to in chapter three) presents first-rate examples of just what can be done when one combines deep primary-source immersion with general hypotheses (in these cases, in relation to the question of why violence is worse and nastier in some conflict settings than in other, apparently analogous ones). In terms of future research trends, it seems to me that we probably need fewer future studies of, say, the First or Second World Wars as such, than attempts to assess how far the specific causes of (for example) the start of one of those conflicts might inform (or challenge, or refine, or demolish) a general argument about the reasons for major wars commencing more broadly. In a related field, my own previous attempt to explain Irish nationalist particularity against an argument about the dynamics of nationalism as such (in my book, *Irish Freedom*) represents one effort to avoid lapsing either into sheer particularism or into de-contextualized, unhistorical generalization.

A second problem, and a related research opportunity and imperative, lies in the disjunction identified on numerous occasions in this book between what people claim or remember about war, and the actual historical reality. Reasons given for going to war (Britain in 1914) very often at best partially overlap with true motivation; reasons for people fighting in the wars once these have begun, are often ennobled misleadingly in the wake of conflict (as with the 1939–45 Allies supposedly having fought because they were committed to protecting Jews from Hitler); our notion that revolutionary violence has been necessary or decisive in providing liberation from oppression frequently involves crass simplification (as in the case of the end of the British Empire); claims from apologists of empire (the British case will suffice again) that militarily-backed hegemony will bring deep benefits to the colonized, again often evaporate on painful inspection; even the patterns of very famous wars can be misrepresented in persistent fashion (as with the trench lenses through which we still tend too often to read the First World War).

Humility in face of these repeated disjunctions again offers rich rewards for future research, less into the mismatch between perception and reality than in terms of explaining why the disjunction *is* so repeated, and why we *do* find it so hard to be honest about war, about why it occurs, about why we fight in it, about what the experience is like in truth, and about what wars do or do not achieve.

One aspect of the emerging research here might, perhaps, involve a reinforcing of the need for long and honest historical memories as we anticipate *future* war (something of importance if scholarship is to have any practical value). How many first-rate historians of Afghanistan or of Iraq thought that what was set out by Washington in, respectively, 2001 and 2003 as the likely trajectory in those two wars and post-war settings was genuinely likely to come to fruition? How many? Another, related dimension might turn out to be that the contingency and complexity of soldiers' motivations and of war-time experience make teleological readings of future (and past) war deeply suspect.

Third, I think that research into modern war should be more honest not merely about the fact that non-state terrorism represents a sub-species of war, but more significantly that so much of what is done in orthodox warfare itself is inherently terroristic. Many will prefer to continue to separate war from terrorism, and there are many reasons for this (some of them good). But the use of terrorizing violence for political ends has again and again emerged as part of what happens in modern war, and—as Fellman and others have argued—there are strong reasons for recognizing that the word 'terrorism' is too narrowly deployed if used only to refer to non-state groups and non-war contexts.

Centrally, there is the matter of historical, analytical honesty. It is simply not true to suggest that state practices in war do not frequently involve the conscious use of terrorizing violence, violence known to possess terrorizing effect, and violence which is simultaneously directed at expressly political ends. There are very many cases throughout the modern era of precisely this phenomenon, of states self-consciously using terrorizing violence for political ends during war, and of those involved in prosecuting

war on behalf of a state seeing it explicitly as just such a process—
one which involves the use of terrorizing violence for political ends
(a process evident in many of the fine books alluded to in these
pages, including those by Kershaw, Ball, Burleigh, and Strachan
and Scheipers). So it is not merely that states self-consciously use
terror against rebels and protesters (though they do), nor just that
states have allied with non-state terrorists when it has suited their
political interests to do so. It is also that what actually happens
when states wage war is itself so often terroristic, and that states
use such violence self-consciously, for political ends, in and as an
integral part of what we rightly call war. Much of what happens in
war is violence which deserves the title of terrorism, from
Hiroshima and Nagasaki in 1945 to the 'Shock and Awe' attack on
Iraq in 2003 by the USA and its allies, to much of the material
which has been discussed in this short book.

Honest acknowledgement of this point in our future framing of
research might also yield practical benefits, perhaps. For there can
be a danger that segregating the terms 'terrorism' or 'terrorist
violence' away from state engagement in war, helps us to close our
eyes to the awfulness of so much warfare, especially that waged by
our own state. As such, it immunizes us from full reflection on the
nature of what we do (or of what is done in our name), and it
probably makes that violence more likely as a result. It might be
that some of that violence is indeed necessary and legitimate: if so,
let us acknowledge what the violence actually involves, let us deny
non-state terrorist adversaries the argument that we are
myopically hypocritical, and let us be sufficiently honest about the
terroristic nature of what we will do to make ourselves absolutely
sure that such violence really is as essential and beneficial as we
(or our political representatives) claim it to be.

A particular version of this point concerns civilian targets, often
seen as definitive of terrorism but as being less so of war. In reality,
as reflected in this book, states have targeted civilians repeatedly
in orthodox war. There could even be a danger (as Zehfuss has

hinted) that the elaborate pretence that 'war' does not target civilians deliberately and intentionally—that civilians have a supposed non-combatant immunity in warfare—might actually allow for war to seem more acceptable and legitimate and justified; that war is thus misrepresented and sanitized as a space within which civilians are not intentionally targeted; and that more people might suffer as a result.

One can still denounce (in my view, more legitimately and authoritatively and credibly denounce) terrorist violence by non-state groups which target civilians if one is honest about what one's own state has done; indeed, if such honesty led to greater restraint in state violence against civilians, then both the generation of and the justification for terrorism would arguably be weakened very considerably. It is the mixture of state callousness towards civilian victims, and hypocrisy about not admitting what is actually being done by states in so much of war, which actually lends terrorist groups the little credibility which they sometimes do possess.

Even leaving aside the deliberate targeting of civilians (and I myself do not think that terrorism necessarily involves this practice), being honest in our future research about the fact that so much modern war has been and remains terroristic in nature would encourage us to be even more hesitant about endorsing or engaging in war. This might perhaps make us more effective in responding to non-state terrorism too. It might be uncomfortable to admit that much that was done in Afghanistan and Iraq as part of the War on Terror did itself involve terrorizing violence practised by the US and the UK. But it is no less true for that. And, in terms of countering non-state terrorism, it is probable that avoiding the Iraq War would have helped the Allies' progress in Afghanistan, both in practical terms of logistics and expertise, and also in terms of retaining credibility in fighting terrorism internationally.

Should we, then, redefine our definition of war, to incorporate 'terrorism' explicitly as part of it? I don't think that this is necessary, since the point is not that all war is terroristic, but rather that terrorism frequently forms an inherent part of war. Rethinking our understanding of war—making clear in our conceptual and analytical approach to future research that terrorism so often constitutes part of what is done during warfare—would help us to understand more fully, to remember more accurately, and to behave more cautiously in relation to the future of the phenomenon of Modern War.

References

Where work has been quoted from or referred to directly, it will be
listed for the chapter in which such quotation or reference first
occurs. Items marked with an asterisk are those which might prove
particularly valuable in further reading on modern war.

Introduction

C. von Clausewitz, *On War* (Harmondsworth: Penguin, 1968; 1st edn
1832).*

R. English, *Armed Struggle: The History of the IRA* (London: Pan,
2012; 1st edn 2003).

—— *Irish Freedom: The History of Nationalism in Ireland* (London:
Pan, 2007; 1st edn 2006).

—— *Terrorism: How to Respond* (Oxford: OUP, 2009).

M. Howard, *Captain Professor: A Life in War and Peace* (London:
Continuum, 2006).

V. Jabri, *War and the Transformation of Global Politics* (Basingstoke:
Palgrave Macmillan, 2007).

Chapter 1: Definition

J. Black, *War: An Illustrated History* (Stroud: Sutton, 2003).*

P. Hirst, *War and Power in the 21st Century* (Cambridge: Polity Press,
2001).

M. Howard, *Clausewitz: A Very Short Introduction* (Oxford: OUP,
2002; 1st edn 1983).

M. Kaldor, *New and Old Wars: Organized Violence in a Global Era* (Cambridge: Polity Press, 2001; 1st edn 1999).

S. Malesevic, *The Sociology of War and Violence* (Cambridge: Cambridge University Press, 2010).*

H. Sidebottom, *Ancient Warfare: A Very Short Introduction* (Oxford: OUP, 2004).

H. Strachan and S. Scheipers (eds), *The Changing Character of War* (Oxford: OUP, 2011).*

M. van Creveld, 'Technology and War I: to 1945' and 'Technology and War II: Postmodern War?' in C. Townshend (ed.), *The Oxford Illustrated History of Modern War* (Oxford: OUP, 1997).

H. G. Wells, *Mr Britling Sees It Through* (London: Odhams Press, n.d. [1916]).

Chapter 2: Causation

H. Arendt, *The Origins of Totalitarianism* (New York: Schocken Books, 2004; 1st edn 1951).

S. Ball, *The Bitter Sea* (London: Harper Press, 2010; 1st edn 2009).

G. Blainey, *The Causes of War* (New York: Free Press, 1988; 1st edn 1973).

R. Dawkins, *The God Delusion* (London: Transworld, 2007; 1st edn 2006).

R. English and C. Townshend (eds), *The State: Historical and Political Dimensions* (London: Routledge, 1999).

J. Goodwin, *No Other Way Out: States and Revolutionary Movements, 1945–1991* (Cambridge: Cambridge University Press, 2001).

A. Gregory, *The Last Great War: British Society and the First World War* (Cambridge: Cambridge University Press, 2008).

D. Kahneman, *Thinking, Fast and Slow* (London: Penguin, 2011).

S. N. Kalyvas, *The Logic of Violence in Civil War* (Cambridge: Cambridge University Press, 2006).*

I. Kershaw, *The End: Hitler's Germany, 1944–45* (London: Penguin, 2011).

M. Kurlansky, *Non-Violence: The History of a Dangerous Idea* (London: Jonathan Cape, 2006).

D. D. Laitin, *Nations, States, and Violence* (Oxford: OUP, 2007).*

D. A. Lake, *Hierarchy in International Relations* (Ithaca: Cornell University Press, 2009).

B. L. Montgomery, *The Memoirs of Field-Marshal The Viscount Montgomery of Alamein* (London: Companion Book Club, 1958).

A. Offer, 'Costs and Benefits, Prosperity, and Security, 1870–1914' in A. Porter (ed.), *The Nineteenth Century (The Oxford History of the British Empire: vol. iii)* (Oxford: OUP, 1999).

F. Partridge, *A Pacifist's War* (London: Robin Clark, 1983; 1st edn 1978).

S. Pinker, *The Better Angels of Our Nature: The Decline of Violence in History and Its Causes* (London: Penguin, 2011).*

P. Preston, *The Spanish Holocaust: Inquisition and Extermination in Twentieth-Century Spain* (London: HarperPress, 2012).

P. Roth, *Nemesis* (London: Jonathan Cape, 2010).

A. Sen, *The Idea of Justice* (London: Penguin, 2009).

P. Shirlow, J. Tonge, J. McAuley, and C. McGlynn, *Abandoning Historical Conflict? Former Political Prisoners and Reconciliation in Northern Ireland* (Manchester: Manchester University Press, 2010).

L. Tolstoy, *War and Peace* (Harmondsworth: Penguin, 1957, two volumes; 1st edn 1865/1869).

T. Tovy, 'Peasants and Revolutionary Movements: The Viet Cong as a Case Study', *War in History*, 17/2 (2010): 217–30.

W. Walker, *A Perpetual Menace: Nuclear Weapons and International Order* (London: Routledge, 2012).

B. F. Walter, *Reputation and Civil War: Why Separatist Conflicts Are So Violent* (Cambridge: Cambridge University Press, 2009).

J. M. Weinstein, *Inside Rebellion: The Politics of Insurgent Violence* (Cambridge: Cambridge University Press, 2007).

A. Wolfe, *Political Evil: What It Is and How To Combat It* (New York: Alfred A. Knopf, 2011).

For Aiken quotation, see Frank Aiken to all Volunteers on Hunger Strike, 5 November 1923, Ernie O'Malley Papers, Archives Department, University College Dublin, P17a/43. For Wall's comments, see *Times* 5 July 2012.

Chapter 3: Lived experience

P. Beaumont, *The Secret Life of War: Journeys Through Modern Conflict* (London: Harvill Secker, 2009).

B. Bond (ed.), *The First World War and British Military History* (Oxford: OUP, 1991).

J. Buchan, *Memory Hold-the-Door* (London: Hodder and Stoughton, 1940).

N. Ferguson, *The Pity of War 1914–1918* (London: Penguin, 1998).*

D. Garnett (ed.), *Selected Letters of T. E. Lawrence* (London: Reprint Society, 1941; 1st edn 1938).

M. Hastings, *All Hell Let Loose: The World at War 1939–1945* (London: HarperPress, 2011).

J. Heller, *Catch-22* (London: Corgi, 1964; 1st edn 1961).

E. Hemingway, *A Farewell to Arms* (Harmondsworth: Penguin, 1935; 1st edn 1929).

E. Hobsbawm, *Interesting Times: A Twentieth-Century Life* (London: Penguin, 2002).

M. Howard, *The First World War: A Very Short Introduction* (Oxford, OUP, 2007; 1st edn 2002).

S. Junger, *War* (London: Fourth Estate, 2010).

K. McLoughlin, *Authoring War: The Literary Representation of War from the* Iliad *to Iraq* (Cambridge: Cambridge University Press, 2011).

G. Orwell, *Homage to Catalonia* (Harmondsworth: Penguin, 1966; 1st edn 1938).

S. Robson, *The First World War* (London: Longman, 1998).

J. Stallworthy (ed.), *The Oxford Book of War Poetry* (Oxford: OUP, 1988; 1st edn 1984).

C. Townshend (ed.), *The Oxford Illustrated History of Modern War* (Oxford: OUP, 1997).*

T. K. Wilson, *Frontiers of Violence: Conflict and Identity in Ulster and Upper Silesia, 1918–1922* (Oxford: OUP, 2010).

For Lessing quotation, see Hastings, *All Hell Let Loose*.

Chapter 4: Legacies

J. Argomaniz, *The EU and Counter-Terrorism: Politics, Polity and Policies after 9/11* (London: Routledge, 2011).

C. Barnett, *The Audit of War: The Illusion and Reality of Britain as a Great Nation* (London: Papermac, 1987; 1st edn 1986).

S. Barry, *A Long Long Way* (London: Faber and Faber, 2005).

P. L. Bergen, *The Longest War: The Enduring Conflict Between America and al-Qaida* (New York: Free Press, 2011).

E. Berman, *Radical, Religious and Violent: The New Economics of Terrorism* (Cambridge: MIT Press, 2009).

T. Blair, *A Journey* (London: Hutchinson, 2010).

A. Brahimi, *Jihad and Just War in the War on Terror* (Oxford: OUP, 2010).

J. Burke, *The 9/11 Wars* (London: Penguin, 2011).

M. Burleigh, *The Third Reich: A New History* (London: Macmillan, 2000).

—— *Moral Combat: A History of World War II* (London: HarperPress, 2011; 1st edn 2010).

E. Chenoweth and M. J. Stephan, *Why Civil Resistance Works: The Strategic Logic of Nonviolent Conflict* (New York: Columbia University Press, 2011).

M. Connelly, 'The Ypres League and the Commemoration of the Ypres Salient, 1914–1940', *War in History*, 16/1 (2009): 51–76.

M. Crenshaw, *Explaining Terrorism: Causes, Processes and Consequences* (London: Routledge, 2011).

S. Croft, *Culture, Crisis, and America's War on Terror* (Cambridge: Cambridge University Press, 2006).

L. K. Donohue, *The Cost of Counterterrorism: Power, Politics, and Liberty* (Cambridge: Cambridge University Press, 2008).

J. B. Elshtain (ed.), *Just War Theory* (New York: New York University Press, 1992).

P. Fussell, *The Great War and Modern Memory* (Oxford: OUP, 2000; 1975).*

R. E. Goodin, *What's Wrong with Terrorism?* (Cambridge: Polity, 2006).

W. R. Gray, *Embedded: A Marine Corps Adviser Inside the Iraqi Army* (Annapolis: Naval Institute Press, 2009).

M. Guidolin and E. La Ferrara, 'The Economic Effects of Violent Conflict: Evidence from Asset Market Reactions', *Journal of Peace Research*, 47/6 (2010): 671–84.

S. Hewitt, *The British War on Terror: Terrorism and Counter-Terrorism on the Home Front Since 9/11* (London: Continuum, 2008).

E. Hobsbawm, *Age of Extremes: The Short Twentieth Century 1914–1991* (London: Penguin, 1994).

—— *Globalization, Democracy, and Terrorism* (London: Little, Brown, 2007).

R. Jackson, L. Jarvis, J. Gunning, and M. Breen Smyth, *Terrorism: A Critical Introduction* (Basingstoke: Palgrave Macmillan, 2011).

S. G. Jones, *Counterinsurgency in Afghanistan* (Santa Monica: RAND, 2008).

T. Judah, *Kosovo: What Everyone Needs to Know* (Oxford: OUP, 2008).

M. Longley, *Collected Poems* (London: Jonathan Cape, 2006).

S. Mendus, *Politics and Morality* (Cambridge: Polity Press, 2009).

J. Mueller and M. G. Stewart, *Terror, Security, and Money: Balancing the Risks, Benefits, and Costs of Homeland Security* (Oxford: OUP, 2011).

D. Omand, *Securing the State* (London: Hurst, 2010).

L. Richardson, *What Terrorists Want: Understanding the Terrorist Threat* (London: John Murray, 2006).

A. Roberts and T. Garton Ash (eds), *Civil Resistance and Power Politics: The Experience of Non-Violent Action from Gandhi to the Present* (Oxford: Oxford University Press, 2009).

M. Scheuer, *Osama bin Laden* (Oxford: OUP, 2011).

E. Stepanova, *Terrorism in Asymmetrical Conflict: Ideological and Structural Aspects* (Oxford: Oxford University Press, 2008).

J. Thompson (ed.), *The Imperial War Museum Book of Modern Warfare: British and Commonwealth Forces at War 1945–2000* (London: Pan, 2003; 1st edn 2002).

M. Walzer, *Just and Unjust Wars: A Moral Argument with Historical Illustrations* (New York: Basic Books, 2006; 1st edn 1977).*

P. Wilkinson, *Terrorism Versus Democracy: The Liberal State Response* (London: Routledge, 2006; 1st edn 2001).

J. Zulaika, *Terrorism: The Self-fulfilling Prophecy* (Chicago: University of Chicago Press, 2009).

For Obama quotation, see *Guardian*, 3 May 2011. For Richards quotations, see *Times*, 24 November 2011. For Carleton-Smith quotation, see *Daily Telegraph*, 6 October 2008. For Manningham-Buller comments, see *Daily Telegraph*, 21 July 2010. For Scheuer comments, see *Guardian*, 3 May 2011. For Miliband comments, see *Guardian*, 15 January 2009. For Colin Powell comments, see *Guardian*, 17 February 2011.

Conclusion: war, terrorism, and future research

M. Fellman, *In the Name of God and Country: Reconsidering Terrorism in American History* (New Haven: Yale University Press, 2010).

G. Greene, *The Third Man* (Harmondsworth: Penguin, 1971; 1st edn 1950).

M. Zehfuss, 'Killing Civilians: Thinking the Practice of War', *British Journal of Politics and International Relations*, 14/3 (2012): 423–40.

Index

Revolution in Military Affairs (RMA) 13
revolutions against the state 31
Richards, General Sir David 94–5
Richardson, L. 100
Robson, S. 60, 85
Roth, P. 46–7
Russia
  part in First World War 41
  part in Second World War 50–51

S

Sarajevo assassinations 37–8
scale 10, 11–12
Scheuer, M. 100
Second World War (1939–45)
  achievements 72
  bombings 62–3
  causes 42
  ending 49–50
  legacies 77
  loss of lives 71
  memories 82
  motivation of individuals 46–7
  number of deaths 61
self-determination 27
  pursuit of 73–4
Sen, A. 55
Serbia 73–4
  part in the First World War 38–9
Sevastopol 8
shared characteristics, factors in nationalism 18–21
Sheehan, M. 101–2
Shirlow, P. et al. 49
Sidebottom, H. 6
size of wars 9
sovereignty 22
  of state 29
Spanish Civil War (1936–9) 46, 68
stalemates as endings 48–9

states 28
  definition 28–9
  formation of new 73–4
  possible links with war 29–32
strategy 16, 27
struggle, nationalist 21–2, 23–4
subordination of states 32
suicide attacks 101

T

tactics 9, 16
Taliban regime 89, 93–7
technology in defining modernity 8–9
territory 19
terrorism 37–8
  9/11 attacks 88, 101–2
  as a sub-set of war 116–19
  war against 88–111
Tolstoy, L. 43–4
torture 104–6
Tovy, T. 47
Townshend, C. 28–9, 61
transport networks 8

U

Ulster 62–4
United Kingdom, counter-terrorism 92–111
United Nations 55–6
United States
  imposed peace 56
  subordinate states 32
  War on Terror 88–111
Upper Silesia 62–4
USA PATRIOT Act 103, 106

V

victories as endings 48
Viet Cong (VC) 47
Vietnam War, motivation of individuals 47

violence
  affected by availability of
    material resources 64–5
  decline 52–7
  relative strength of
    boundaries 62–4

W

Walker, Charles Rodger 65–7
Walker, William 54
Wall, Sir Peter 56
Wallenstein 9
Walter, Barbara 27, 33
Walzer, Michael 84
War and Peace (Tolstoy) 43–4
War on Terror 88–111
warfare as sub-set of war 6

weapons of mass destruction
  (WMDs) 97–9, 109
Weinstein, Jeremy 42, 64, 114
Wells, H. G. 60
Wilkinson, P. 99
Wilson, Tim 62–4, 114
Wolfe, Alan 36, 43, 57, 74
Wolfowitz, Paul 109
women, opportunities for 78

Y

Ypres, Belgium 80

Z

Zehfuss, M. 117–18
Zulaika, Joseba 90

SOCIAL MEDIA
Very Short Introduction

Join our community
www.oup.com/vsi

- Join us online at the official Very Short Introductions **Facebook** page.
- Access the thoughts and musings of our authors with our online **blog**.
- Sign up for our monthly **e-newsletter** to receive information on all new titles publishing that month.
- Browse the full range of Very Short Introductions online.
- Read **extracts** from the Introductions for free.
- Visit our library of **Reading Guides**. These guides, written by our expert authors will help you to question again, why you think what you think.
- If you are a teacher or lecturer you can order inspection copies quickly and simply via our website.

Visit the Very Short Introductions website to access all this and more for free.
www.oup.com/vsi

ONLINE CATALOGUE
A Very Short Introduction

Our online catalogue is designed to make it easy to find your ideal Very Short Introduction. View the entire collection by subject area, watch author videos, read sample chapters, and download reading guides.

http://fds.oup.com/www.oup.co.uk/general/vsi/index.html